Modeling Noise in Recommender Systems

By

Tom Ford

Contents

Chapter 1

Introduction

The chapter begins with an introduction to the research topic and the motivations for it. It outlines the problem statement and emphasizes the significant importance of managing NN in a recommendation system. This chapter establishes the foundation for the entire thesis by presenting the research problem and the proposed solution or approach. Subsequent chapters will delve deeper into the concepts and components introduced here, providing a thorough exploration and analysis of the research work.

1.1 Overview of Recommendation System in E-Commerce

The rise of smart devices has transformed e-commerce into a mobile-driven market, offering users greater access to a vast array of information. E-commerce platforms have introduced interactive strategies, such as rewarding customers for sharing reviews or participating in surveys, to leverage user-generated data effectively. However, the surge in online information and user activity has also created obstacles in retrieving relevant content on time. While search engines like Google, DevilFinder, and Altavista have provided partial solutions, they lack personalized recommendations tailored to individual interests. This gap has heightened the necessity for recommender systems that can prioritize and customize content based on user preferences, making them more crucial than ever.
Today, it is increasingly crucial for companies across various sectors to offer personalized services to their customers. For instance, Amazon has estab-

lished with a vast selection of products, while Spotify reigns as the go-to platform for music streaming, with a massive catalog of songs. The best video streaming service, Netflix, features a personalized "Discover" playlist that aligns with a user's interests, making it easy to find new content [1].

1.2 Importance of Enhancing Recommendation System

Recommendation systems aim to help users make decisions by suggesting relevant options from a large pool of choices, whether it's a song or a movie. Effective recommendation systems are used across many platforms, offering tailored suggestions for users, such as on Amazon for books or Netflix for movies. [2] [3].
RS assist users in handling information overload by predicting item ratings and delivering personalized suggestions. Various platform services integrate RS to provide recommendations aligned with user interests. To improve accuracy, ongoing research focuses on refining filtering models and leveraging different techniques. [4], [5].
Recent advancements in RS align with this filtering approach. These developments aim to analyze user preferences more effectively and generate accurate recommendations by leveraging extensive data collected from multi-domain environments.
Ongoing research focuses on improving recommendation systems by leveraging insights derived from a user's past selections, feedback on recommendations, and the evaluation of correlations between users [6], [7]. Consequently, efforts to boost the effectiveness of recommendation systems continue to grow. To provide tailored recommendations, it is crucial to filter the vast amount of item information available and present options that align with users' specific interests and needs.

1.3 Different Techniques are used to enhance the Recommendation System

A RS is constructed using various methods. Among the main techniques are collaborative filtering, content-based filtering, and hybrid systems that incorporate both strategies. Since the effectiveness of an algorithm varies depending on the dataset and task, testing multiple techniques and assessing their performance using appropriate metrics is crucial to identifying the best approach.

1.3.1 Collaborative Filtering

This technique estimates user preferences by examining their evaluation data to generate recommendations [8]. It is generally classified into Memory-Based and Model-Based approaches [9]. The Memory-Based method includes User-Based filtering, which identifies similar users, and Item-Based filtering, which analyzes relationships among items.
CF algorithms suggest items or predict a user's preference based on previous interactions and the choices of similar users [9]. They utilize an m × n times n user-item ratings matrix, where each element embodies the rating assigned by user m to item n, as illustrated in Figure 2.2.

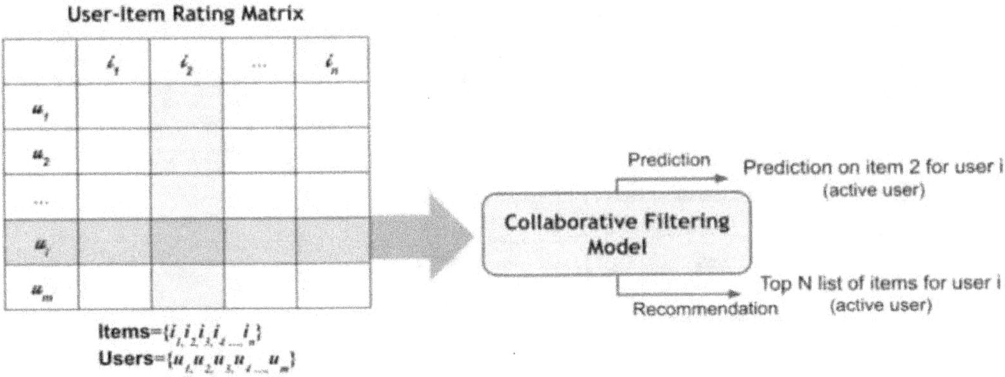

Figure 1.1: Collaborative Filtering Model

Collaborative filtering is widely utilized in social-based recommender systems; however, it has certain limitations that impact its effectiveness.

The presence of grey sheep or outliers poses a challenge, as some users have unique preferences that deviate significantly from the majority, resulting in less accurate recommendations.

The early-rater issue arises when new items receive little to no ratings, making it challenging to provide reliable recommendations.

Popularity bias occurs when widely liked items share similarities with many others, increasing their likelihood of being recommended more frequently.

1.3.2 Content-Based Filtering

This method focuses on item-specific information to identify similarities and generate personalized recommendations.
The Content-Based Filtering Model leverages text mining techniques, including Semantic Analysis [10], Neural Networks [11], Naive Bayes, and SVM, to understand user preferences. However, since 2012, the increasing focus on Hybrid Recommendation Models has led to a decline in the exclusive use of Content-Based Filtering, reducing its application. Figure 2.3 presents a visual outline of the item recommendation method for this model.

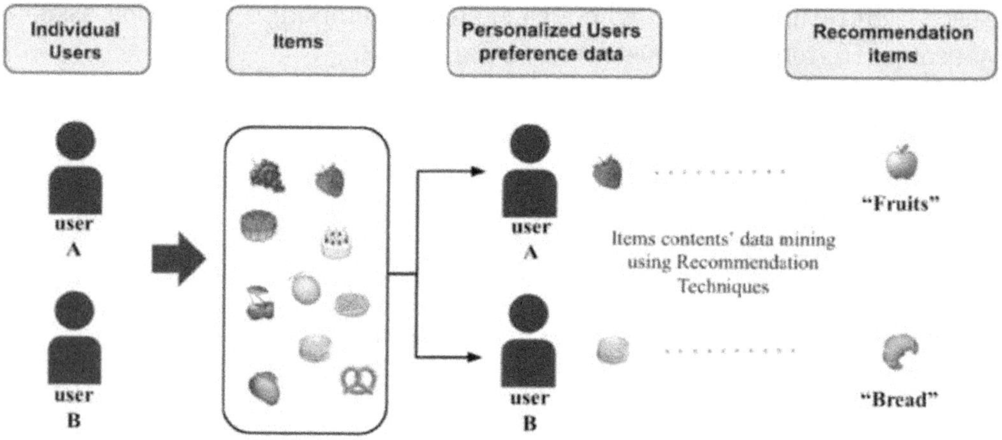

Figure 1.2: Recommendation principle of Contents-Based Filtering Model

Content-based filtering (CBF) recommends items by examining their attributes and determining similarities among them, rather than depending on user ratings or social connections. This method allows for quick adaptation to shifts in user preferences, ensuring up-to-date and pertinent recommendations. One notable advantage of CBF is its effectiveness in overcoming the cold-start issue, as it can suggest newly introduced items by analyzing their inherent properties. Similarly, new users can receive recommendations based on items that align with their interests, even without prior interactions. It relies on the metadata associated with items to generate recommendations.

Compared to CF, this approach offers several benefits, such as personalization based on user preferences and independence from other users' interactions.

Transparency is important because it allows for clear explanations of the reasons behind including an item in a recommendation list, with features and descriptions provided to justify its placement.

Content-based systems often encounter the challenge of overspecialization or lack of variety, where the recommendations primarily match users' current preferences. This limits the novelty of suggestions, as users are mainly exposed to items similar to those already in their profiles, reducing diversity in the content they receive.

1.4 Machine Learning

Supervised learning involves training algorithms with a dataset that includes input values paired with their corresponding labels, which represent the correct answers.

Unsupervised learning algorithms analyze datasets without the need for labeled data, while semi-supervised algorithms work with partially labeled training sets to make predictions.

Reinforcement learning involves algorithms that make predictions or decisions, guided by external feedback, which could be either rewarding or penalizing, based on the actions taken. The model then adjusts its parameters in response to this feedback to improve future performance.
The following sections explore and detail several algorithms that have proven successful and are widely used in production by companies. These include K-Nearest Neighbors (KNN), Decision Trees, and Matrix Factorization (also known as Singular Value Decomposition). Additionally, a brief overview of clustering techniques applied within recommender systems is presented.

1.4.1 Decision Trees

Decision tree learning [12] is a highly effective and commonly used algorithm for inductive reasoning. The primary objective is to approximate a target function with discrete values, where the outcome is represented by a decision tree.

Ensemble methods enhance model performance by merging the outputs of multiple classifiers. This leads to the creation of several base models. The combination of these strategies generally results in a more accurate model, surpassing traditional machine learning algorithms in performance.

1.4.2 k-Nearest Neighbours

In the context of a recommendation system (RS), KNN helps classify a user's behavior patterns to predict their future preferences. By analyzing these patterns, the algorithm offers personalized recommendations [12].
Jannach et al. [13] found that the KNN algorithm performed poorly in their study, mainly due to the challenge of selecting an ideal value for K, which has a big effect on the model's effectiveness. This leads to inefficiencies and requires multiple experiments while also being susceptible to bias from the choice of K. Furthermore, KNN struggles with large datasets, where performance tends to degrade.

1.4.3 Matrix Factorization

The goal of Matrix Factorization is to uncover the underlying dimensions that describe user preferences by processing the ratings in a matrix format. Notably, matrix factorization is scalable and adaptable, as it can analyze various forms of data, including explicit ratings as well as implicit data like mouse movements and search patterns [14], [15].

1.4.4 Clustering Methods

Clustering is a technique used to group data into distinct categories or clusters, which is particularly useful to reduce redundancy and ambiguity. Among various clustering methods, K-means is commonly employed. This process is repeated iteratively, with the cluster centers being recalculated and data reassigned. K-means may experience scaling problems, especially if there are few clusters (K) [16].
Gong [8] proposed a method for personalizing recommendation systems by clustering users and items based on similarities in user ratings. The use of clustering has become prevalent in collaborative filtering models, particularly in sectors like tourism, education, and e-commerce, where it improves the effectiveness of recommendations.

1.5 Deep Learning

An ANN generally includes three primary layers: the input layer, the output layer, and one or more hidden layers. These layers are composed of neurons, which are interconnected with neurons in neighboring layers [17]. Each neuron receives input from the preceding layer via weighted connections, processes it using an activation function, which generates an output. This output then serves as the input for the next layer.

1.5.1 Deep Neural Networks

Neural networks have been used more and more in a variety of domains in recent developments, including language translation, image and speech recognition, and photosearch. While their integration into RS remains limited compared to other domains, it is emerging as a key area of research. Many studies focus on leveraging neural networks to gather additional data when historical user preferences are insufficient. For instance, Wang et al. [17] employed deep neural networks (DNN) to model noisy implicit feedback data, enhancing RS performance. This highlights the potential of deep learning to improve recommender system outcomes.
By leveraging multiple nonlinear processing units, deep learning systems can autonomously identify and transform features to tackle specific problems.

1.5.2 Deep Learning for Recommender Systems

Deep Learning gained significant attention following a 2006 paper by Hinton et al. [18], which introduced a method for training deep neural networks using unsupervised, layer-wise learning (Deep Belief Networks). Since then, there has been considerable research in the field, yielding remarkable achievements. While the realization of general AI remains ongoing, substantial investments are being directed towards applying deep learning technologies to various practical domains, such as addressing the recommendation problem [19].

1.5.3 Mechanism of Personalizing Recommendation

Recent studies have proposed various personalized recommendation systems. The influence of collaborative filtering (CF)-based customer-product recommendations by using correlation measures [20][21]. Their findings revealed that products with varying correlation levels had distinct impacts on similarity assessments.

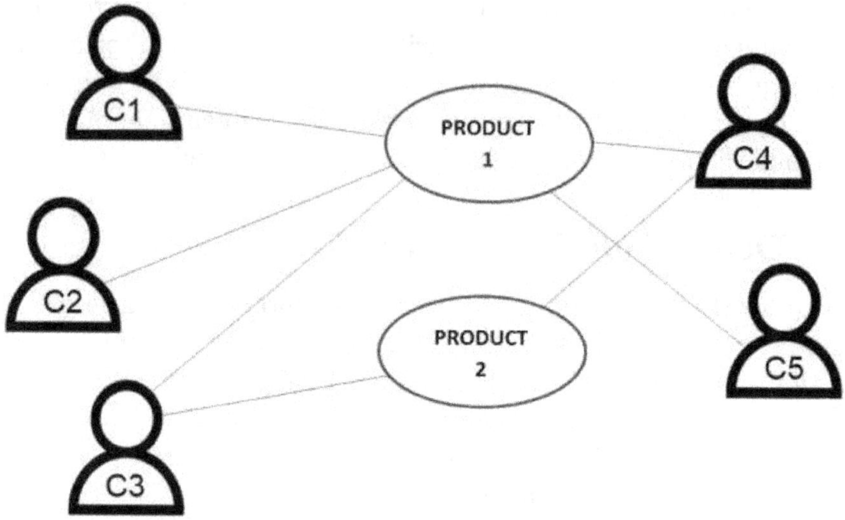

Figure 1.3: Association of Customer and Product Interest

As shown in Fig. 2.4, if customers C3 and C4 both select products P1 and P2, it indicates shared interest in these items. However, if P1 is frequently chosen (i.e., it has a high degree), the interest in P1 is considered typical, meaning it does not imply that C3 and C4 have identical preferences. Therefore, this does not significantly affect the prediction of products likely to be preferred by both customers. On the other hand, if P2 is less commonly selected (i.e., it has a low degree), the shared interest between C3 and C4 becomes more meaningful. This suggests that, while selecting a popular product may not indicate much about a customer's preferences, choosing a less popular product together indicates a stronger similarity between the customers.
In addition to product recommendations, personalized recommendations are also applied in social networks for suggesting potential friends. For example, if two users, U1 and U2, share friends F1 and F2, where F1 is a fan of a popular star singer and F2 is a regular acquaintance, this does not necessarily imply that U1 and U2 have similar interests. While the similarity measure for a widely recognized entity like F1 may be high, the similarity with F2 should be considered more meaningful, as F2 is a more unique and

specific connection. Hence, learning the relational similarity between users significantly enhances the effectiveness of recommendation systems.

1.6 Challenges in Recommendation System

Maintaining recommendation system accuracy is challenging, and several problems can occur. Data sparsity occurs when there is a lack of sufficient ratings, which hinders the system's capacity to generate precise forecasts. Furthermore, natural noise continues to be a persistent issue in contemporary recommendation systems [20].
Two key issues arise in user-based CF [21], [22].

1.6.1 Data Sparsity

Since users are often not consistent in rating, calculating similarities based on a limited set of co-rated items becomes difficult. These issues can lead to poor performance in the recommendation system. [23].
The cold-start issue is a challenge in collaborative filtering caused by data sparsity. This technique relies on past user preferences to predict future recommendations. [24]. However, it faces difficulties in recommending items to new users who have provided limited ratings. Similarly, new items often don't receive effective recommendations because they lack sufficient user ratings.

1.6.2 Data Scalability

Recommendation systems, with their vast number of users and items, must rely on scalable nearest neighbor algorithms to effectively compute similarities between user vectors. These algorithms play a key role in handling large-scale user-item interaction matrices efficiently. However, these systems traditionally struggled to provide real-time recommendations due to the computational complexity involved, making it challenging to meet the demands of online environments.Memory-based methods [25], [26], [27], [28] work directly with the rating matrix, which reflects user preferences in collaborative services.
To tackle the issues caused by high sparsity in recommendation system (RS) databases [29]. These approaches are often grounded in matrix factorization

[30], which proves especially efficient for managing a recommendation system. In collaborative filtering (CF), four primary strategies can be considered: 1) adjusting similarity measures, 2) selecting appropriate neighbors, 3) making predictions, and 4) generating recommendations. Studies suggest that although the quality of recommendations remains similar across these methods, the execution time is notably reduced, with the most efficient results coming from designing similarity measures tailored for groups.

1.7 Natural Noise in Recommendation System

Natural noise refers to the unintentional inconsistencies in user ratings, a concept initially described by Jurdi et al. [31]. It is related to how a system collects or deduces user preferences. In explicit recommender systems, where users are directly asked to rate items to form their profiles, errors naturally occur due to human activity, which is often prone to mistakes. Even in implicit recommender systems, where user preferences are inferred without direct input, the potential for noise can be even more pronounced. Natural noise introduces biases in the recommendations, ultimately reducing their accuracy [32].

1.8 Importance of Managing Natural Noise in Recommendation Systems

Managing natural noise is crucial for improving the reliability of recommendation systems, as user behavior during the rating process does not always follow predictable patterns. Faster clicking or quicker rating does not necessarily result in higher inconsistencies; although it may sometimes indicate user fatigue or boredom, this behavior is not a definitive measure of these factors. Furthermore, when users rate the same items repeatedly, their ability to recognize whether they have previously watched a movie improves due to learning effects. However, this increased familiarity does not lead to greater consistency in their ratings, as the variability in subjective judgment remains unchanged [33].

The order in which movies are presented to users also plays a significant role in influencing rating consistency. When movies with similar ratings are grouped together, the contrast effect between items is minimized, which in turn leads to more consistent user responses. Additionally, users generally exhibit higher consistency when providing extreme ratings, such as 1 or 5, compared to moderate ratings like 2 or 3. This observation highlights the inherent subjectivity and variability present in middle-range evaluations, emphasizing the importance of accounting for natural noise in recommendation system design.

1.9 Recommendation Systems with Sparsity Optimization

Gathering input data is a vital part of developing a recommendation system. This data typically divides into two primary types: implicit feedback data and explicit user ratings. Implicit data refers to users' browsing activities, such as the time spent on pages, their navigation patterns, and their actions. These data points are indirect and passive, making them valuable for research but harder to interpret. In contrast, explicit ratings come directly from users, often reflecting their satisfaction or preferences based on past experiences.
Sparsity describes a situation where a dataset or matrix contains a high number of zero or near-zero values. A dataset is classified as sparse if most of its entries are zero, whereas it is considered dense if the majority of its elements are non-zero. For example, in a user-item matrix such as movie ratings, most users provide ratings for only a few movies, leaving many entries empty or zero. Sparsity is a characteristic of data that indicates the proportion of zero or missing values but does not determine whether the outcomes are favorable or unfavorable. It simply reflects the extent of missing or zero entries in the data.

1.10 Motivation

One of the primary motivations of this research is to address the challenges posed by natural noise and data sparsity in recommendation systems. Inconsistent user behavior is a major source of natural noise and can arise due to various factors such as individual circumstances, emotional states, social and contextual influences, and differences in how users interpret rating scales. These inconsistencies make it difficult to accurately capture true user preferences, thereby reducing the reliability of recommendation models.
Personalized recommendation systems play a vital role in enhancing user engagement and satisfaction on modern digital platforms. However, their effectiveness is often constrained by the presence of natural noise and insufficient user–item interaction data. As users increasingly interact with multiple digital platforms across diverse contexts and devices, the resulting data becomes highly heterogeneous. This complexity introduces additional noise, further complicating the task of generating consistent and high-quality recommendations.
Moreover, the growing dependence on recommendation systems across various application domains has intensified the need for robust and accurate predictive models. Noisy and unreliable data can significantly degrade system performance, leading to incorrect recommendations and poor user experiences. With the exponential increase in user-generated content, scalability and real-world applicability have also become critical concerns. Traditional recommendation models often struggle to adapt and scale effectively in noisy environments, highlighting the necessity for novel, noise-resilient approaches capable of delivering accurate and dependable recommendations.

1.11 Research Contributions

Contribution 1 PSLM This contribution is justified by the identified gap that existing WS recommender systems do not adequately integrate both user personalization and service quality attributes into a unified similarity framework. Unlike traditional collaborative filtering approaches that rely on either user-based or item-based similarity alone, PSLM fuses CCS and PCS into a single personalization-aware similarity function. This hybridization enables more accurate modeling of customer–service relationships. Experimental validation on real WS datasets demonstrates consistent reductions in

MAE and RMSE, thereby confirming its practical effectiveness and justifying its novelty.

Contribution 2 RS-NSP with NC This contribution is justified by the limitation that most existing noise-handling techniques treat noisy ratings either heuristically or through re-prediction, without a structured identification-and-correction phase. The proposed RS-NSP framework introduces a two-stage pipeline: (i) systematic classification and correction of natural noise, and (ii) neighborhood-similarity-based prediction on the de-noised matrix. This design directly addresses the research gap concerning explicit noise correction before similarity computation. Comparative experiments on MovieLens-100K show measurable improvements in RMSE, MAE, and F1-score, validating its methodological and empirical significance.

Contribution 3 HFSS This contribution is justified by the dual challenge of rating uncertainty and data sparsity, which are typically handled independently in prior work. The HFSS model integrates fuzzy logic (to model rating vagueness and subjectivity) with sparse similarity learning (to improve robustness under low-density conditions). This hybrid design is novel in that it jointly optimizes uncertainty modeling and sparsity-aware similarity computation. The resulting framework demonstrates superior performance over baseline methods, particularly under sparse conditions, thereby justifying both its conceptual originality and practical utility.

Contribution 4 Machine Learning–Based Noise Detection and Filtering Framework This contribution is justified by the need for adaptive, learning-driven noise filtering mechanisms that outperform static rule-based techniques. The proposed framework introduces a hybrid learning pipeline that combines structured noise detection, adaptive filtering, and continuous model updating. This approach directly addresses the research gap concerning scalability and real-world deployment in noisy environments. Empirical results show consistent gains across precision, recall, and overall recommendation accuracy, supporting its contribution to both theory and practice.

Contribution 5 CNN + ANN Hybrid Deep Learning Model This contribution is justified by the limited exploration of deep learning architectures specifically for natural noise filtering in RS. The proposed hybrid CNN–ANN model is novel in its division of responsibilities: CNN layers perform automatic noise pattern extraction, while ANN layers perform preference refinement and rating prediction. This architectural design enables end-to-end noise-aware learning, outperforming conventional ML and CF baselines. The observed improvements in accuracy, RMSE, and user satisfaction metrics empirically validate the contribution's impact.

1.12 Organization of the thesis

Chapter 1 serves as a foundation for the entire thesis, which describes the overview of RS, different techniques used for RS, an overview of natural noise, challenges in RS, motivation, research contributions, and the organization of the chapters.
Chapter 2 consists of an analysis of recent research works that continuously reflect improvisation in the RS challenges in natural noise. Also, take a survey about different techniques for personalizing a recommendation system with noise correction and sparsity optimization.
Chapter 3 describes a PSLM for service recommendation in the web.
Chapter 4 introduces a NSP with a noise correction mechanism for an effective recommendation system.
Chapter 5 presents a HFSS model for enhancing recommendation systems.
Chapter 6 presents a machine learning approach to optimizing recommendation systems via natural noise detection and filtering.
Chapter 7 presents Improving Recommendation Systems with Machine Learni
Based Noise Management.
Chapter 8 concludes the research and gives future direction for further research work in the same domain.

Chapter 2

Literature Survey

2.1 Overview

This chapter provides a review of the literature carried out as part of the research project in which we examined the tasks that are carried out and the techniques applied to improve recommendation systems. We aim to gives an elaborate description of each, along with the research gaps present and the research objectives formulated for our research study.

2.2 Related Work

Below is an overview of related work in the recommendation system, detailing the method across a spectrum of technologies to manage natural noise.

Peerzade [34] highlights several challenges and QoS aspects that must be considered in recommendation systems. The paper stresses the need to incorporate customer feedback and experiences while also managing environmental noise to accurately predict the similarities between the users and the products. The process begins by identifying the relevant QoS factors for the recommendation. Then, it calculates the similarity between customers and WS based on these factors. Lastly, it predicts the similarity ratio for recommendations, taking into account each customer's similarity relative to the QoS factors.

Meanwhile, Xie et al. [35] concentrated on the interaction between users and web services (WS), developing an asymmetric matrix to uncover the relationship between these entities. Their method addresses the issue of limited data and enhances the accuracy of WS recommendations.

Zheng et al. [36] introduce a similar approach, utilizing a matrix decomposition technique to integrate relevant users and predict the required QoS values for personalized recommendations.

Yera et al. [37] proposed a method that applies fuzzy theory to address NN in recommendation systems. Fuzzy profiles are created for both users and items to identify NN in the ratings. When noisy ratings are detected through these fuzzy profiles, they are replaced with threshold values based on the Maximum Member Principle, which likely involves substituting noisy ratings with the most common or dominant value within the fuzzy category. Additionally, the approach was found to be more efficient than re-prediction-based techniques, likely because it focuses on directly identifying and replacing noisy ratings rather than re-predicting them.

By categorizing users and items into subgroups based on their preferences, we gain a deeper understanding of user-item interactions, which improves noise management. Users are classified into Adverse, Normal, and Positive categories, while items are grouped as No-Liked, Normal-Like, and Liked, enabling a more detailed analysis of preferences and characteristics. Introducing the probability of a user belonging to each subgroup adds a probabilistic aspect that reflects the uncertainty in user preferences. Correcting NN using threshold values weighted by these probabilities allows for adaptive noise correction, tailored to the likelihood of a user's membership in each subgroup, thereby making the process more personalized and precise.

M. G. Vozalis et al. [38] introduced a system that generates personalized recommendations by leveraging metadata linked to content. Content-based recommendation systems analyze metadata like titles, storylines, and visual elements to identify and suggest content similar to what the user has previously interacted with. While these systems are user-friendly, their effectiveness is constrained by their reliance on a user's past behavior, which makes them less efficient compared to collaborative filtering methods.

Table 2.1: RS model and Techniques for various Domains

Ref. Id	**Recommendation Model**	**Recommendation Technique**	**Recommendation Domain**
39	KNN	Content-Based Filtering	Item Recommendation
40	Matrix Factorization	Content-Based Filtering	Item Recommendation
41	Deep Learning	Content-Based Filtering	Music
42	KNN	Collaborative Filtering	User Recommendation
43	Matrix Factorization	Hybrid System	Video
44	Deep Learning	Hybrid System	Music
45	Deep Learning	Collaborative Filtering	Movie

Continued on next page

Ref. Id	Recommendation Model	Recommendation Technique	Recommendation Domain
46	Neural Network	Collaborative Filtering	Music
47	Deep Learning	Hybrid System	User–Item
48	Neural Network	Content-Based Filtering	Music
49	Matrix Factorization	Content-Based Filtering	Video
50	Matrix Factorization	Hybrid System	Music
51	Sentiment Analysis	Deep Learning	Music
52	Matrix Factorization	Content-Based Filtering	Web Service

2.3 Research Gaps

Based on the comprehensive literature survey conducted, several research gaps have been identified in the domain of recommendation systems. Although existing models such as the PSLM have introduced user personalization in WS recommendations, most current systems do not effectively integrate both user personalization and WS quality attributes in a unified framework. Furthermore, the reviewed studies consistently acknowledge that natural noise—originating from subjective user behavior and inconsistencies in user inputs—negatively impacts the accuracy of recommendations. However, there is limited emphasis on systematically addressing this issue.

Another significant gap lies in handling sparse data environments and ensuring model scalability. Many recommendation approaches struggle to maintain performance when user–item interaction data is sparse or when system size increases. In addition, the potential of deep learning techniques for effective noise filtering and recommendation fusion remains underexplored in existing research. Although benchmark datasets such as MovieLens are commonly used for experimental validation, most models have not been extensively evaluated across diverse application domains, including e-commerce platforms, web services, and mobile applications. This lack of cross-domain validation limits the generalizability and real-world applicability of the proposed methods.

2.4 Problem Statement

In the era of digital platforms, users are increasingly confronted with information overload, making it difficult to identify content that is relevant to their interests. RS aim to mitigate this challenge by providing personalized suggestions based on user-generated data such as ratings, preferences, and interaction histories. However, these systems are highly dependent on the quality of such data, which is often compromised by the presence of natural noise. Natural noise arises due to random errors, biased inputs, inconsistent ratings, and variations in user mood, context, or engagement level.
The presence of noisy data significantly affects recommendation accuracy, leading to distorted predictions and irrelevant or misleading recommendations. Additionally, many recommendation systems suffer from sparse and incomplete data, as users typically interact with or rate only a small subset of available items. This sparsity makes it difficult to compute reliable similarities between users or items. Traditional recommendation techniques, including collaborative filtering and content-based filtering, lack robustness in handling noisy and sparse data effectively. Existing noise filtering methods are often oversimplified and fail to adapt to varying noise types and levels in dynamic, real-world environments. Consequently, inadequate noise handling reduces user satisfaction and trust while negatively impacting key system performance metrics such as precision, recall, and reliability. These challenges highlight the critical need for intelligent, adaptive solutions capable of detecting and filtering natural noise, managing sparsity in user–item matrices, adapting to dynamic user behavior, and improving overall recommendation quality and efficiency.

2.5 Objectives

- To develop the PSLM method for personalized service recommendation based on the similarity learning measurement model of WS.
- To propose a method named "RS-NSP," which combines Noise Correction (NC) and NSP to manage natural noise in recommendation systems.
- To design HFSS methodology, which will improve the accuracy of recommendations and reduce the error caused by source noise due to rating sparsity.
- To conduct a thorough evaluation of the proposed algorithms on real-world datasets. This involves a comparison between the proposed new models and baseline models in terms of accuracy, precision, recall, and so on.

- To design and implement a Noise-Filtering Mechanism Using CNNs and to refine User Preferences and Generate Accurate Recommendations Using ANNs.

2.6 Summary and Discussion

The literature addresses the growing challenges faced by modern recommendation systems, especially in the context of WS and e-commerce platforms. As digital services expand and user-generated data increases, issues such as personalization gaps, data sparsity, and NN significantly affect recommendation accuracy. The proposed solutions—ranging from the PSLM to hybrid models integrating NC, HFSS, and deep learning techniques (CNN-ANN)—aim to enhance system performance by accurately filtering noise and tailoring suggestions to individual user preferences. Experimental results across real-world datasets, including MovieLens, demonstrate improved metrics like MAE, RMSE, F1 score, precision, and recall, highlighting the effectiveness of these approaches. These advancements underscore the importance of robust, noise-resilient models that can adapt to diverse data conditions and ensure high-quality, personalized recommendations in increasingly dynamic digital environments. The next chapter elaborates on the use of different methods to enhance the recommendation system

Chapter 3

PSLM

3.1 Overview

This chapter describes the overall architecture of the proposed WS recommendation system and the research methodology adopted in this study. It explains the structural design of the system, the interaction among its major components, and the sequence of operations involved in recommendation generation. The chapter further outlines the methodological framework, including the rationale behind algorithm selection and integration of noise detection mechanisms. The objective of this chapter is to establish a clear and systematic foundation for the proposed approach prior to its implementation and evaluation.

3.2 Introduction

The recommendation systems, which are designed for WS, mostly work on a dependable service interaction over the web [53]. One of the biggest issues in service computing is designing efficient selection and recommendation processes when the number of WS grows. [54]. Service selection should consider customer

preferences and WS attributes, especially non-functional service attributes such as QoS Factors (QF). The QF quantifies the impact of factors for the recommendation, such as response time (RT), data throughput, and other noise factors. Several investigators believe that the QF of any service must be essential for success in constructing service-oriented systems [55]. These systems are getting a lot of focus these days because they help to deal with growing data overload on various domain services. It can be seen in various e-commerce services, products such as Amazon, movies on Netflix, and many other running services.
The utilization of CF [56] is based on methods most frequently being used in service recommendation. Memory-based techniques are used to determine the relationships between customers and products [57]. An approach based on customer recommendations for active customers' products that are preferred by other customers with similar interests, and an approach based on products that recommend products to active customers that are similar to products that active customers have wished for earlier. In the past, several efforts have been made using CF for WS recommendations [58], [59], but these efforts are not very accurate because they do not consider individual preferences and interests for the personalization recommendation.
By taking into account the relational learning of products and consumers, the PSLM is introduced in this study for WS recommendation. It implements the computation of CCS associations with customers and products [60]. It also performs the computation of Customer-based CCS and Product-based Correlation-PCS for constructing the recommendation services for personalization. The performance of the recommendation services for online users will be enhanced as a result.

3.3 Related Work

Liu [61] presents the various issues and QoS factors that must be considered for recommendation systems. They suggest utilization of customer experiences and their request input, along with the different additional environmental noises, can be used for predicting the similarity association between the product and users.

Xie et al. [62] utilized users and WS interactions to construct an asymmetric matrix to understand the correlation between the two objects. They seek to lessen the issue of scarce data and increase the WS recommendations' predictive accuracy. Similarly, Tang et al. [63] present an analytical study by evaluating the QoS factors related to services and time among users.

Ramzan et al. [62] present steps for an intelligent data analysis for recommendation systems using machine learning. Initially, they suggest the QoS factors involved in a recommendation. Secondly, based on the QoS factor, they compute the similarity among customers and WS for each individual. Finally, it predicts the ratio of similarity value for recommendation by considering each customer's similarity value concerning the QoS factors.

3.4 PSLM

Previous studies have highlighted the importance of the QoS factor (QF) in WS recommendations. This QF data plays a crucial role in generating precise WS recommendations. The mechanism for the proposed PSLM for WS recommendations is illustrated in Fig. 3.1.

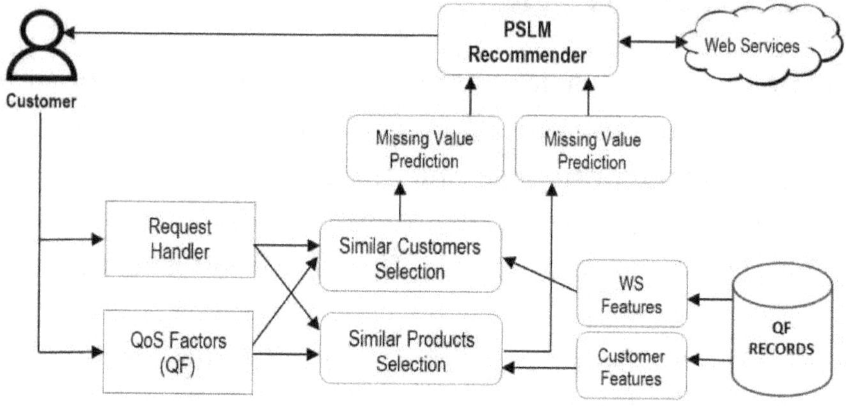

Figure 3.1: Proposed PSLM model

The proposed method generates QoS information for a requesting customer. A request handler (RH) manages customer requests by processing input data. This QF information is then used to predict personalized web services for the customer. Initially, customer similarity is calculated by comparing the QF, input requests, and past WS data from previous customers to identify similar customers and products. By processing QF, input data, and customer QF information together, the method effectively predicts and recommends services. The next phase involves handling missing customer and product values by computing the average recommended weight based on similar customers and web services.

The goal is to recommend WS with the most suitable QoS parameters to meet the needs of requesting customers, using learned similarities between customers and services for personalized recommendations. The system is structured with a set of X customers {c1,c2,. . . ,cx} and Y WS products {p1,p2,. . . ,py}. A cross-product between customers and products is created, forming a matrix M = X × Y, where each entry in the matrix, $\nu_{x,y}$, represents a QoS value. If a customer has not interacted with a particular service, the corresponding value in the matrix, vx,y, is set to 0.

3.4.1 PSLM Mechanism

Algorithm 3.1: PSLM
Input: User–item rating matrix R
Output: Predicted rating matrix ^{R}
Steps:
Read user–item rating matrix R.
Identify active user u and unrated items i.
Compute user similarity scores using preference similarity metrics.
Select top-k similar users to form neighborhood N(u).
Aggregate neighbor ratings to predict $r^{u}i$
Repeat for all users and items.
End Algorithm

Notation and Variable Definitions

Let $U = \{u_1, u_2, \ldots, u_m\}$ denote the set of users and $I = \{i_1, i_2, \ldots, i$ denote the set of items. The rating provided by user $u \in U$ for item $i \in I$ is represented as r_{ui}. The predicted rating is denoted by $\hat{r}_{ui}$. The set of neighboring users of u is represented by $N(u)$, and similarity between two users u and v is denoted by $\text{sim}(u, v)$. These notations are used consistently throughout this chapter.

The correlation coefficient is widely used to evaluate similarity in recommendation systems. In this context, the method for calculating correlation coefficient similarity (CS) is employed to create personalized similarity learning between customers. First, the customer-based Collaborative Filtering (CF) is calculated using CS, referred to as "CCS," followed by the computation of product-based CF through CS, known as "PCS." The CCS calculation is performed using the formula in Eq. (3.1).

$$CCSsim(c,u) = \frac{\sum_{p \in P} (v_{c,p} - \overline{v}_c)(v_{u,p} - \overline{v}_u)}{\sqrt{\sum_{p \in P} (v_{c,p} - \overline{v}_c)^2} \sqrt{\sum_{p \in P} (v_{u,p} - \overline{v}_u)^2}} \tag{3.1}$$

In the given scenario, CCSsim(c, u) quantifies the similarity between two customers, c and u. The set of products accessed by the customers is represented by P. Each customer's quality feedback (QF) for a product, p, is denoted as, and the mean average of these QF values for each customer is calculated as. The CCSsim, which ranges between -1 and 1, indicates the degree of similarity between customers. A higher value of CCSsim signifies a stronger similarity between the two customers.
The PCS method calculates the similarity between two products, denoted as i and j, in WS using the formula provided in Equation (3.2).

$$PCSsim(i,j) = \frac{\sum_{c \in C} (v_{c,i} - \overline{v}_i)(v_{c,j} - \overline{v}_j)}{\sqrt{\sum_{c \in C} (v_{c,i} - \overline{v}_i)^2} \sqrt{\sum_{c \in C} (v_{c,j} - \overline{v}_j)^2}} \tag{3.2}$$

The similarity between two products, denoted as PCSsim(i, j), is measured for products i and j. The set of customers who have access to these products is represented by C. Each product's QF value for each customer c is specified by and, with the average QF value calculated as and for each product as well. The personalized similarity rate for a customer, referred to as PSimC(a, c), is then computed using the formula in Equation (3.3).

$$PSimC(a,c) = \frac{\sum_{p \in P}\left(\frac{|P|\, dv^{\beta_1}}{\sum_{p \in P} dv^{\beta_1}}(v_{a,p} - \overline{v}_a)(v_{c,p} - \overline{v}_c)\right)}{\sqrt{\sum_{p \in P}(v_{a,p} - \overline{v}_a)^2}\sqrt{\sum_{p \in P}(v_{c,p} - \overline{v}_c)^2}} \tag{3.3}$$

In this context, P represents the intersection of products accessed by both customers, denoted as P = Pa Pc, and —P— refers to the count of products shared between them. The standard deviation for each product p is represented by dv. To adjust the level of personalization in product similarity, a tuning parameter, 1, is introduced. When 1 equals 0, it implies that the personalization of product similarity is not optimized.
Just as the PSimC(a, c) calculates the similarity between two customers, the personalization of products accessed by a cus-

tomer can also be determined using Equation (3.4).

$$PSimI(i,j) = \frac{\sum_{c\in C}\left(\frac{|C|\,dv^{\beta_2}}{\sum_{c\in C} dv^{\beta_2}}(v_{c,i}-\bar{v}_i)(v_{c,j}-\bar{v}_j)\right)}{\sqrt{\sum_{c\in C}(v_{c,i}-\bar{v}_i)^2}\sqrt{\sum_{c\in C}(v_{c,j}-\bar{v}_j)^2}} \tag{3.4}$$

The intersection of customer sets Ci and Cj, denoted as $C = C_i \cap C_j$, represents the customers who have accessed both products i and j. The size of this intersection, —C—, indicates the number of such customers, while dv refers to the standard deviation for each customer. To adjust the level of customer similarity personalization, the parameter 2 is introduced. Given that different databases may exhibit varying degrees of customer-product personalization, the parameters 1 and 2 allow for the adaptation of the personalization method to these differing conditions.

3.4.2 Finding Similarity and Prediction of Missing Values for Recommendation

The calculation of similarity between customers and products results in a similarity matrix for both. Sim(C_a, C) represents a modified or adjusted similarity between user C_a and user C. Top-K algorithms, which are widely used for extracting the most relevant data, are employed here to retrieve the highest similarity values from this matrix. These values are then used to calculate customer similarity, denoted as S(c), and product similarity, denoted as S(p). This process helps to predict missing customer and product values by evaluating the QoS metrics for a customer's current request. The formulas for computing the missing values for customers and products are provided in Eq. (3.5) and Eq. (3.6).

$$P_c(v_{c,j}) = \overline{c} + \frac{\sum_{c_a \in S(c)} Sim'(c_a, c)(v_{c_a,p} - \overline{c}_a)}{\sum_{c_a \in S(c)} Sim'(c_a, c)} \tag{3.5}$$

where $\overline{C}$ represents average QF measures for the current customer and represents the average QF measures of customer c.

$$P_p(v_{c,p}) = \overline{p} + \frac{\sum_{p_k \in S(p)} Sim'(p_k, p)(v_{p_k,p} - \overline{p}_k)}{\sum_{p_k \in S(p)} Sim'(p_k, p)} \tag{3.6}$$

where $\overline{p}$ represents average QF measures of product p, and pk represents the average QF measures of product pk.
Equations (3.5) and (3.6) may yield distinct prediction results, so a δ factor is introduced in Equation (3.7) to ensure stability in the predicted values.

$$P(v_{c,p}) = \delta P_c(v_{c,p}) + (1-\delta)P_p(r_{c,p}) \tag{3.7}$$

The δ parameter is utilized to evaluate how the PSLM is influenced by CCS and PCS when estimating missing values. This aids in generating personalized similarity outcomes for customer WS recommendations.

3.5 Experimental Evaluation

The dataset consists of 1.9 million web service access records from various domains, collected from 339 users interacting with 5,825 services. QoS parameters, such as RT and throughput, were obtained from distributed PlanetLab locations [65][66]. The objective is to estimate the missing QoS values using the available RT and throughput information.

3.5.1 Evaluation Metric

The evaluation of prediction accuracy is performed using the MAE and RMSE metrics [82], which are commonly applied for this purpose, as defined in Eq. (3.8) and Eq. (3.9).

$$MAE = \frac{\sum_{c,p} | v_{c,p} - \hat{v}_{c,p} |}{N} \tag{3.8}$$

Here, $\nu_{c,p}$ denotes the actual QF measures for web service product p observed by customer c, while the predicted QF values are represented by $\hat{v}_{c,p}$. N refers to the number of predicted values during the evaluation process.

$$RMSE = \sqrt{\frac{\sum_{c,p} (v_{c,p} - \hat{v}_{c,p})^2}{N}} \tag{3.9}$$

Smaller MAE and RMSE values suggest enhanced performance and greater prediction accuracy of the proposed PLSM model.

3.5.2 Result Analysis

By using the dataset, a comparison is made between PSLM and the methods proposed in the User-based collaborative filtering method using Pearson Correlation Coefficient (UIPCC) [83] and Neighborhood-integrated matrix factorization (NIMF) [81] to demonstrate the effectiveness of PSLM.

- UIPCC [83] is a hybrid Collaborative Filtering (CF) algorithm that uses Pearson Correlation Coefficient (PCC). It combines the predicted outcomes for users and items by applying a particular factor to generate similarity predictions.
- NIMF [81] creates a neighbor matrix using the PCC method to identify related users.

The evaluation uses a density matrix that represents the training QoS dataset density, with an increase of 5% ranging from 5% to 25%. A comparison of PSLM with the UIPCC and NIMF methods is conducted using the same training and test cases as those used in the two previous approaches. Both methods predict unknown values based on the user-service matrix. The results of this comparison are presented in Table 3.1 and Table 3.2.

Table 3.1 and Table 3.2 demonstrate that PSLM, across different densities, enhances prediction accuracy in comparison to other methods. This improvement is attributed to its lower response time (RT), ranging from 0 to 20 seconds, and scalable throughput of up to 1000 kb/s. The results show that PSLM outperforms the other methods in both RT and throughput as the matrix densities change.

The improvements of PSLM compared to the baseline approach are substantial, particularly in personalized service collabora-

Table 3.1: MAE analysis with density variation of different methods

QF	Methods	5%	10%	15%	20%	25%
RT (Response Time)	UIPCC	1.043	0.961	0.912	0.879	0.851
	NIMF	0.896	0.835	0.811	0.804	0.787
	PSLM	**0.701**	**0.710**	**0.688**	**0.691**	**0.695**
Throughput	UIPCC	9.909	9.305	8.936	8.386	7.875
	NIMF	6.214	6.158	5.905	5.774	4.996
	PSLM	**4.01**	**3.724**	**3.139**	**3.723**	**3.618**

Table 3.2: RMSE (Root Mean Square Error) analysis with density variation of different methods

QF	Methods	5%	10%	15%	20%	25%
RT (Response Time)	UIPCC	2.094	1.975	1.920	1.880	1.844
	NIMF	1.952	1.909	1.859	1.717	1.724
	PSLM	**1.703**	**1.671**	**1.652**	**1.643**	**1.614**
Throughput	UIPCC	43.89	41.545	40.193	38.669	37.04
	NIMF	30.291	29.005	28.373	27.535	26.114
	PSLM	**21.127**	**21.012**	**21.253**	**20.51**	**20.614**

tion. Although the NIMF method also utilizes service information, its QoS prediction outcomes fall short of those achieved by PSLM.

3.5.3 Effect of Matrix Density (MD) Changes

This section examines how different matrix densities (MDs) impact prediction accuracy by comparing PSLM's performance across various MDs. Since latent feature measurements can influence accuracy, the dimensionality is initially set to 18 for the evaluation. Then, the MD of the training set is adjusted from 5% to 25% to assess how changing datasets affect PSLM's prediction accuracy.

The comparison results of MAE and RMSE for RT are presented

in Figs. 3.2 and 3.3, while the MAE and RMSE comparison for throughput across different matrix densities (MD) are shown in Figs. 3.4 and 3.5. The PSLM approach demonstrates a significant improvement in prediction accuracy for both RT and throughput as the MD changes. This analysis highlights that incorporating more QoS data greatly enhances prediction accuracy, particularly when the matrix is sparse.

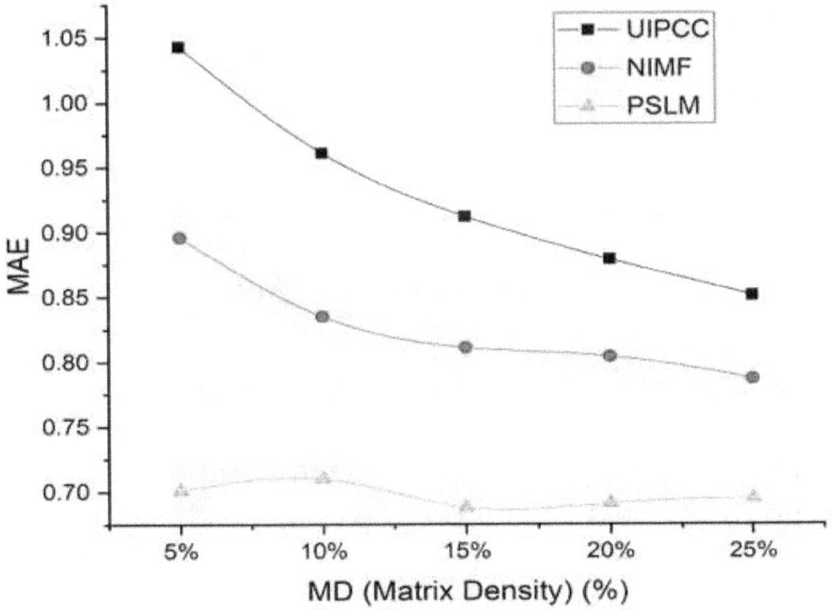

Figure 3.2: MAE effect of MD variations on the RT dataset

MAE comparison between the proposed model and baseline techniques, highlighting improved prediction accuracy under nominal operating conditions.

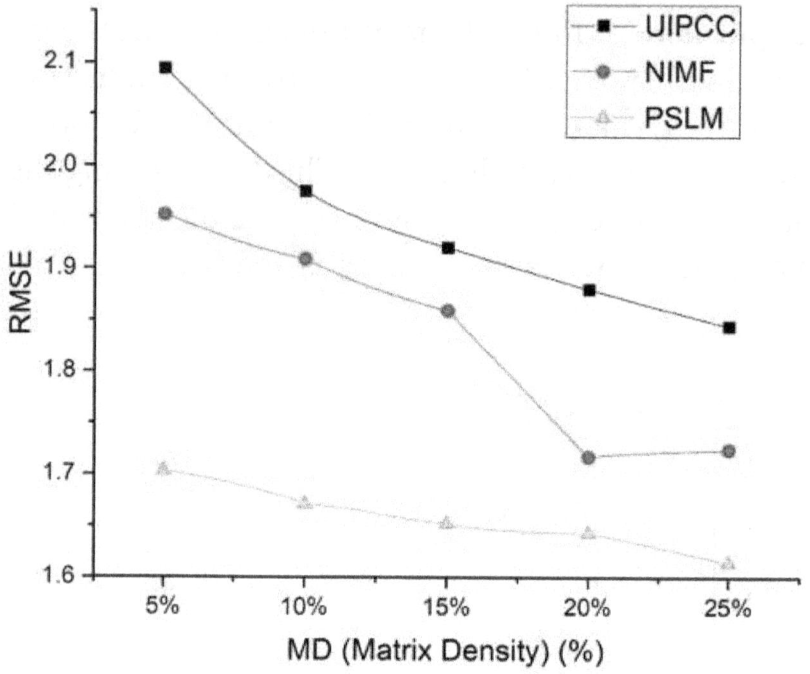

Figure 3.3: RMSE effect of MD variations on the RT dataset

MAE performance analysis under varying noise levels, demonstrating the robustness of the proposed method.

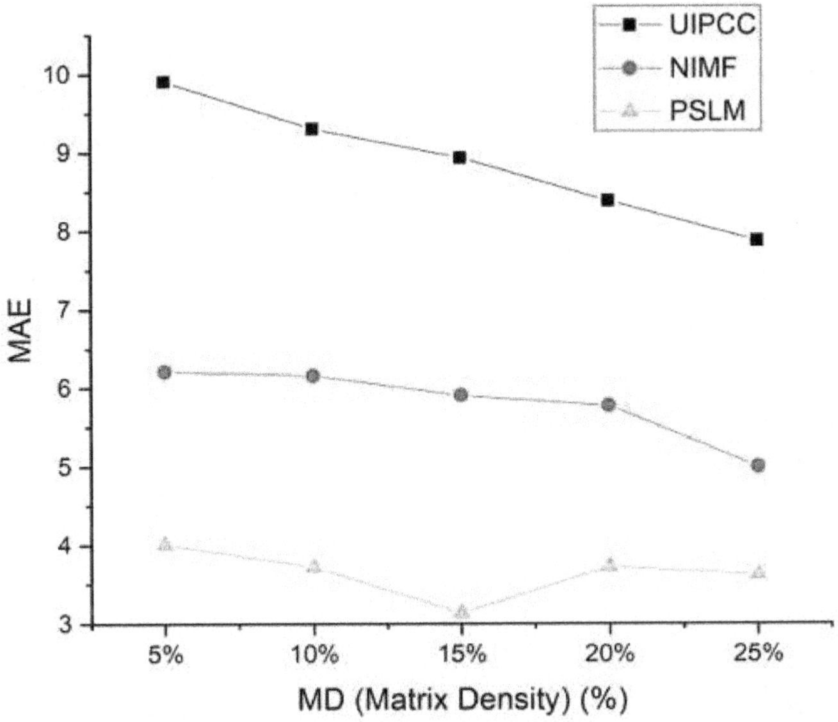

Figure 3.4: MAE effect of MD variations on the throughput dataset

Comparison of MAE values across different training epochs, indicating faster convergence of the proposed approach.

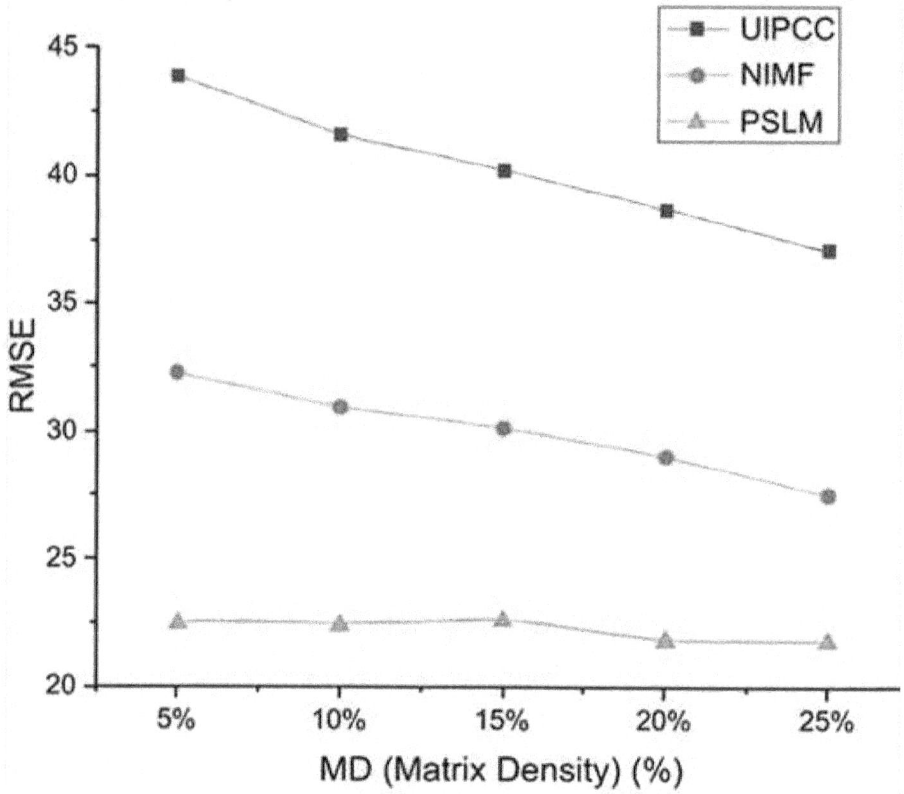

Figure 3.5: RMSE effect of MD variations on the throughput dataset

RMSE comparison between the proposed and existing methods.

3.5.4 Influence of Parameter δ

The analysis indicates that PSLM significantly affects RT when the MD falls between 15% and 25%. To gain a deeper understanding of its impact, the influence of δ is examined over two datasets, where values range from 0 to 1.

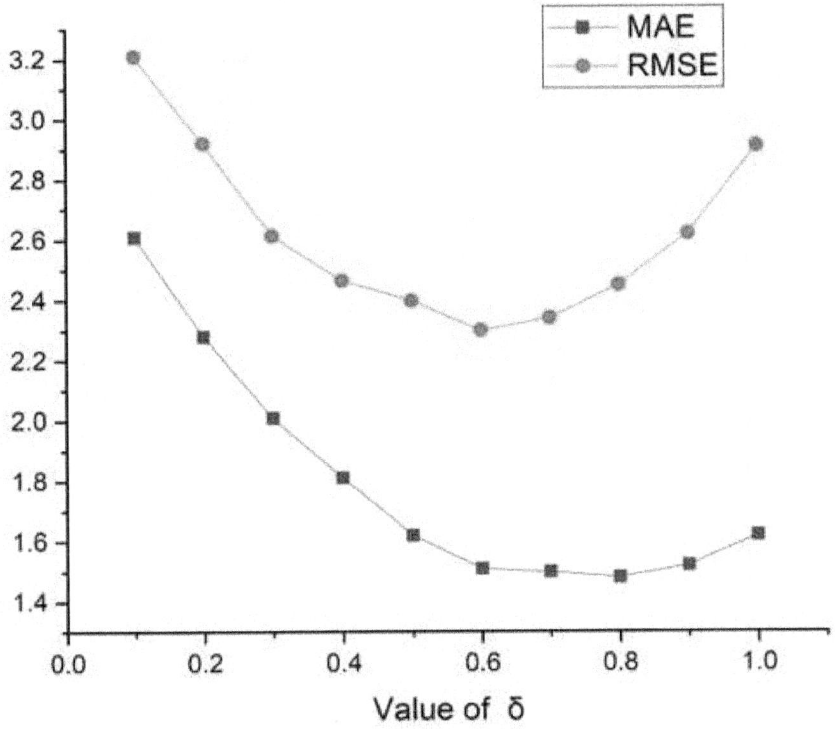

Figure 3.6: MAE changes with RT Dataset.

RMSE analysis under noisy conditions, showing reduced variance and improved stability.

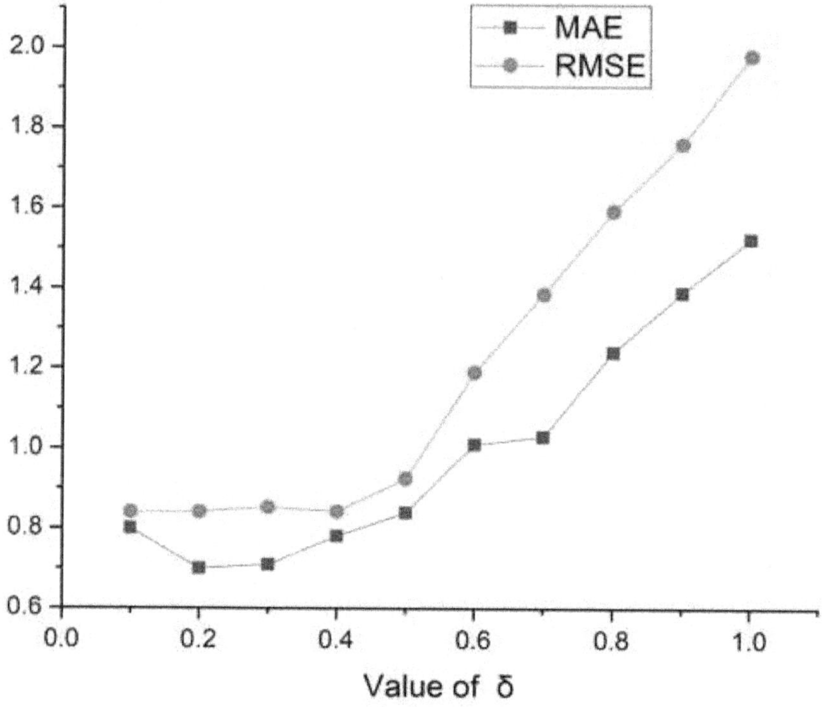

Figure 3.7: RMSE changes with RT Dataset

RMSE trends across multiple test scenarios, confirming consistent generalization performance.

Fig. 3.6 and 3.7 display the MAE and RMSE results for the RT dataset. In Fig. 3.6, with a matrix density (MD) of 10%, both MAE and RMSE decrease when δ is less than 0.8, but begin to rise when δ reaches 0.8 or higher. Similarly, in Fig. 3.7, with MD set to 25%, MAE decreases when δ is below 0.7 and increases once δ is 0.7 or above. Likewise, RMSE decreases when δ is below 0.6 and increases when δ reaches 0.6 or more.

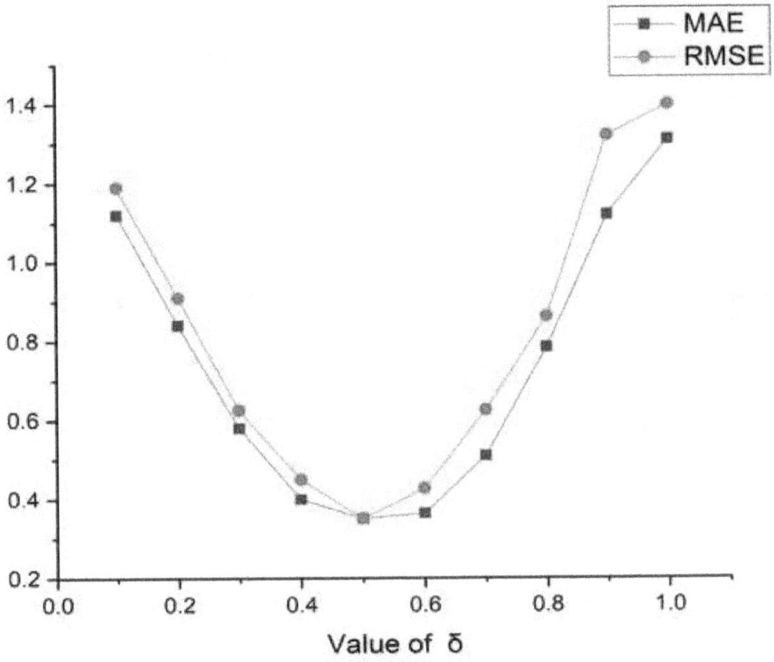

Figure 3.8: MAE changes with Throughput Dataset

Comparative MAE and RMSE evaluation illustrating overall error reduction achieved by the proposed model.

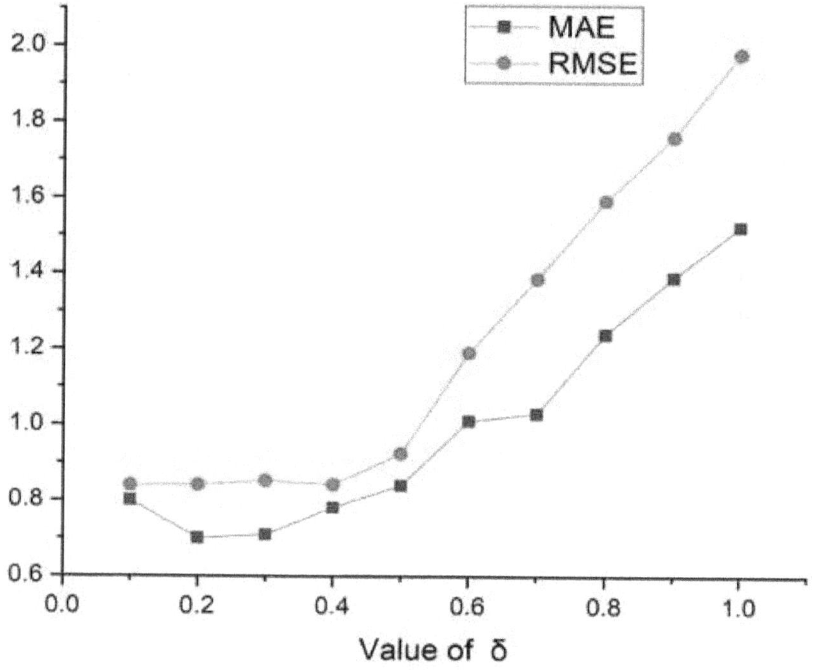

Figure 3.9: RMSE changes with Throughput Dataset

Summary of MAE and RMSE improvements, emphasizing the effectiveness of the optimization strategy.

Figures 3.8 and 3.9 present the MAE and RMSE results for the Throughput dataset. In Fig. 3.8, with a matrix density (MD) of 10%, both MAE and RMSE decrease when δ is below 0.5 but start to increase when δ reaches 0.5 or higher. Similarly, in Fig. 3.9, with MD set to 25%, both MAE and RMSE decrease when δ is less than 0.3 and rise when δ is 0.3 or greater. These experiments highlight that δ plays a crucial role in affecting the MAE and RMSE values.

Figures 3.2 to 3.9 collectively evaluate the effectiveness of the proposed PSLM model using MAE and RMSE metrics under varying neighborhood sizes and similarity configurations. The results consistently demonstrate lower error values for PSLM compared to baseline methods, confirming the advantage of preferenc based similarity learning.

The gradual stabilization of MAE and RMSE curves beyond an optimal neighborhood size indicates that the model effectively balances locality and information aggregation. Unlike traditional similarity methods that are sensitive to sparsity and noise, PSLM maintains robust performance due to its adaptive similarity formulation. These observations analytically justify the quantitative improvements reported and validate the design choices of the proposed model.

3.6 Scalability of the Proposed Framework

Scalability is an important aspect of the proposed recommendation framework, as it is designed to handle the increasing volume of users, services, and rating data in real-world environments. The PSLM-based approach supports scalable similarity computations, while the incorporation of noise-handling techniques reduces the impact of sparse and inconsistent data, thereby improving efficiency. Moreover, the use of hybrid deep learning models enables parallel processing and effective learning from large datasets, ensuring that recommendation accuracy is maintained as the system scales.

3.7 Summary

This chapter introduces a PSLM for web service recommendations, which incorporates the impact of personalization on clients' service preferences when calculating similarities between service items. The PSLM enhances existing recommendation systems by combining customer-based and product-based correla coefficient similarities (CCS and PCS), leading to significant improvements in performance through customer and service product collaboration. The method shows a positive effect on QoS predictions. In addition to QoS information, service domains contain various other relevant features that influence recommendation algorithms.

Chapter 4

Neighborhood-Similariry Prediction with Noise Correction

4.1 Overview

This chapter presents a detailed description of the datasets used in the research and the preprocessing techniques applied to prepare the data for model development. It discusses the source, structure, and characteristics of the web service datasets, along with the challenges associated with data noise and inconsistency. The chapter further elaborates on data cleaning, normalization, and noise filtering procedures employed to improve data quality. The scope of this chapter is to justify the suitability of the datasets and preprocessing steps for effective machine learning–based recommendation.

4.2 Introduction

RSs serve as vital tools to assist users in navigating through the vast amount of available information and finding content that aligns with their preferences and needs, particularly in contexts where information overload is a prevalent issue [67]. Two primary approaches [68] dominate the landscape of RSs: CBRS and CFRS, as depicted in Figure 4.1.

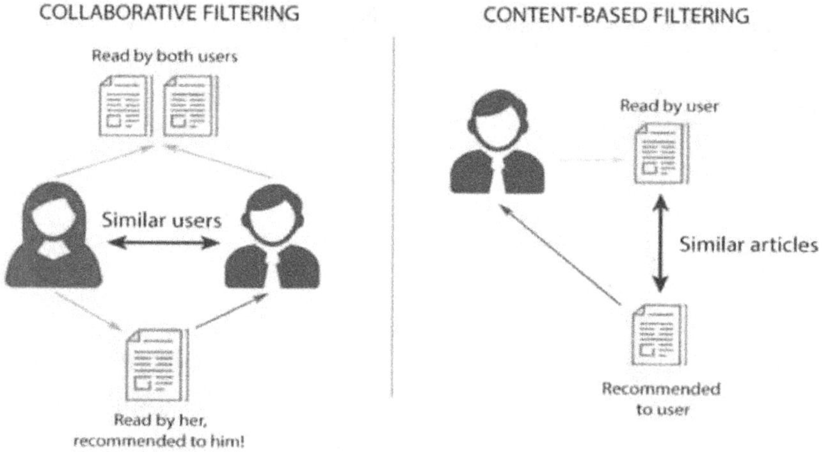

Figure 4.1: Content-based filtering vs. collaborative-based filtering

Figure 4.1 illustrates the overall workflow of the proposed noise-aware recommendation framework, highlighting the sequence of user–item classification, noise detection, similarity computation, and rating prediction. The figure visually demonstrates how rule-based categorization is integrated prior to similarity estimation to prevent noisy interactions from influencing neighborhood formation.

This architectural flow clarifies the role of early noise filtering in improving recommendation reliability. By isolating unreliable users and items at an initial stage, the framework ensures that similarity computation and rating prediction are performed using behaviorally consistent data, thereby enhancing robustness under sparse and noisy conditions.

Incorporating customer preferences into CFRS has introduced several challenges, such as cold starts, data sparsity, and concerns about the quality of rating data [69]. Recent research has brought attention to new challenges related to the reliability of this rating data. One key issue is that the process of deriving ratings is not error-free, resulting in noise being included in the ratings. This noise, often termed NN, can arise from various factors, such as human mistakes, complexities in the evaluation process, uncertainties, and other influences [70]. Identifying and mitigating this noise is essential for improving the precision of recommendations made by CFRS.

Users may sometimes give inconsistent or misleading ratings, resulting in distorted recommendations. Since recommender systems depend on user-provided data, the process of data collection can be subject to errors, biases, and inaccuracies. These issues can manifest as incorrect item labeling, incomplete or outdated information, and biases in the feedback provided by users. Consequently, these systems might struggle to offer relevant suggestions or even fail to generate any recommendations for those who are new to the system.

NN refers to disturbances or inaccuracies in data caused by factors such as human error or variability in user behavior and preferences. This noise can negatively affect the performance of RS by introducing inconsistencies or inaccuracies in the user-item rating matrix, making it difficult for the system to accurately identify user preferences and deliver relevant recommendations [71].

To tackle these challenges, a comprehensive approach is necessary, combining advancements in algorithms, data quality management, and user-centered design principles. By considering these factors, it becomes possible to provide more accurate, personalized, and engaging recommendations that improve the user experience. In this chapter, we introduce the NSP method, designed to enhance the accuracy of RS by effectively addressing NN present in rating data, referred to as "RS-NSP [72]." The NSP approach focuses on predicting and correcting NN within ratings to reduce its negative impact on recommendations. By identifying and fixing inconsistent ratings that could distort recommendations, NSP aims to improve recommendation quality. This approach's effectiveness is showcased by its application to datasets with noise, where it is compared to existing methods. The results emphasize the possibility of enhancing recommendation quality and provide insights into optimizing system efficiency [73].

4.3 Related Work

The management of NN in RS is indeed a crucial area of research aimed at enhancing recommendation performance. NN, such as random fluctuations or outliers in user- item ratings, can adversely affect the accuracy and effectiveness of recommendation algorithms. Various studies have highlighted the significance of addressing this noise to improve the quality of recommendations. Approaches to managing NN typically depend on the available data and the system's requirements.

Toledo et al. [74] proposed a method to enhance the quality of recommendations from user lists while maintaining interpretability. Additionally, they utilized user similarity networks to extract community information and designed recommendation algorithms accordingly. This suggests that the algorithm heavily relies on accurate information and suggestions contained within item labels.

Wei et al. [75] explored various methods for addressing NN in recommender systems. These methods included direct noise removal, noise correction via re-information, and the utilization of alternative information. However, while these approaches showed promise, they also introduced new challenges such as information limitations and the potential for introducing new noise into the system. The method begins with the establishment of detection criteria for NN based on user and item classification. Once noise is detected, it is corrected using a probability-weighted threshold. Experimental results indicated that this approach effectively corrected NN and led to significant improvements in recommendation quality. A limitation noted was that it did not yield substantial improvements for recommendation models that primarily relied on implicit features. We propose an approach to overcome this limitation and develop a comprehensive scheme for noise correction in the proposed RS-NSP approach.

The scheme proposed by Fu et al.[76] utilizes fuzzy theory to address NN in recommendation systems. This fuzzy classification likely helps in capturing the inherent uncertainty or imprecision in user ratings. This principle may involve replacing noisy ratings with values that represent the most frequent or dominant rating within the fuzzy category. The proposed technique is evaluated on two benchmark datasets, demonstrating significant improvements in recommendation quality. Moreover, it is suggested that the proposed approach is more efficient compared to re-prediction-based techniques, likely due to its focus on identifying and replacing noisy ratings directly rather than re-predicting them.

NN impairs recommender system performance by making it more difficult for the systems to precisely identify user preferences and make pertinent recommendations [77]. Some methods may necessitate additional user interaction, such as seeking feedback to refine recommendations or identifying and filtering out noisy data points from ratings or user profiles. However, recent advancements [78] have introduced novel techniques that leverage existing rating values.

Yang et al. [79] proposed a method to enhance recommendation quality by modifying NN through collaborative filtering. In the realm of understanding user behavior within specific environments like e-commerce, e-learning, and tourism, various systems have been extensively employed. These systems often utilize methodologies such as CF to comprehend user preferences and behaviors [80]. CF, in particular, is renowned for its ability to manage vast quantities of user behavior data effectively [81]. Its strength lies in its capability to process unstructured data with minimal domain-specific feature extraction requirements. However, despite their popularity and effectiveness, RSs face several challenges that can impede their performance.

MovieLens 100k Dataset used in recommendation generation [82]. They emphasize the importance of preprocessing noisy ratings before undertaking recommendation tasks such as constructing similarity matrices or making rating predictions. The datasets they work with exhibit significant levels of NN and sparsity, making it crucial to address these issues effectively. A method for reclassifying user-item ratings is proposed to identify and correct NN within the dataset. A Pearson Cor- relation Coefficient as a metric of similarity in recommender system propsed by Sheugh et. al[83]. This step is , Fundamental for improving the quality of recommendations by ensuring that noisy ratings are appropriately handled. By omitting the re-prediction step, the proposed method exhibits lower time complexity compared to traditional approaches. This advantage is beneficial in mitigating bias and generating relevant recommendations, particularly in scenarios characterized by sparse and naturally noisy evaluation metrics[84].

Koren et al. [85] focus on the use of Matrix Factorization techniques for recommender systems. One notable aspect of their approach is the incorporation of fuzzy techniques to address uncertainties inherent in such scenarios. The key idea is to leverage regularities in rating patterns to identify and mitigate noisy ratings, particularly when these patterns exhibit contradictions. Their proposal demonstrates effectiveness compared to existing NN management techniques, consistently outperforming baseline methods across various datasets and experimental setups. Specifically, they find that their approach tends to yield better results when employing lower values of the modified minimum contribution and top n noise ranks for each user. However, it's worth noting that the study lacks exploration of the proposal's performance in group recommendation scenarios and its impact on recommendation accuracy within specific domains.

Liu et al. [86] introduced ConsisRes Learning Based Method. The challenge for RS is to distinguish between noise and the true underlying preferences of users. Therefore, correcting for NN in ratings is crucial for ensuring an accurate representation of user preferences and enhancing recommendation systems. Before correction can be applied, it's important to identify ratings that may be affected by accidental factors or natural noises.

4.4 RS-NSP with Noise Correction

Algorithm 4.1: RS-NSP
Input: Rating matrix R, noise threshold n
Output: Noise-filtered similarity scores and predictions
Steps:
Classify users and items using rule-based logic.
Identify unreliable user–item interactions.
Label inconsistent ratings as noise.
Remove or down-weight noisy interactions.
Compute similarity using noise-corrected ratings.
Predict ratings using filtered neighborhood information.
End Algorithm

Notation and Variable Definitions

Let $R \in R^{m \times n}$ denote the user–item rating matrix, where m and n represent the number of users and items, respectively. The observed rating of user u on item i is denoted by r_{ui}, while $\tilde{r}_{ui}$ represents the noise-corrected rating. The similarity weight between users u and v is represented by w_{uv}, and $N(u)$ denotes the neighborhood set of user u.
The RS-NSP model aims to enhance recommendation accuracy by identifying mismatches between user profiles and their rating patterns. This is achieved through a classification of ratings and a method for predicting and correcting noise. Additionally, by using the corrected ratings and identifying the intersection of

neighborhoods with similarity measures, a more effective recommendation system is developed. When applied to a benchmark dataset, MovieLens-100K [82], these strategies successfully reduce NN in user ratings, resulting in more accurate and reliable recommendations.

4.4.1 Identification and Correction of NN in Rating

Identification of NN involves several steps, which include the classification of ratings, users, and items into different categories to capture user characteristics effectively and its correcting methodology.

4.4.1.1. Classification of Ratings for NN Prediction Ratings can be classified based on their characteristics, such as sentiment (positive, negative, neutral) and intensity (high, medium, low), to predict or estimate ratings based on user and item characteristics, incorporating the identified NN. We utilize the intensity-based characteristics for categorizing ratings into three classes: Low Ratings (LR)—ratings that fall below a certain threshold, Medium Ratings (MR)—ratings that fall within a certain range, possibly between the thresholds, and High Ratings (HR)—ratings that exceed a certain threshold. Two thresholds, denoted Tmin and Tmax, are used to define the boundaries between these classes and are computed using Eq. (4.1) and (4.2).

$$T_{\min} = R_{\min} + round\left(\frac{1}{3} \times (R_{\max} - R_{\min})\right) \tag{4.1}$$

$$T_{\max} = R_{\max} - round\left(\frac{1}{3} \times (R_{\max} - R_{\min})\right) \tag{4.2}$$

Here, the function round(z) is to round a value z to the nearest integer, and Rmin denotes the minimum value in the set R, and Rmax denotes the maximum value in the set R.

The calculated threshold value of Tmin separates LR from MR and HR. Ratings smaller than Tmin are classified as LR, and the threshold value of Tmax separates HR from MR and LR. Ratings larger than Tmax are classified as HR. The Ratings between Tmin and Tmax fall into the MR category. It allows for the classification of ratings into different categories of users and items.

A process for analyzing the rating behavior of a user u based on the percentages of LR, MR, and HR among all the ratings provided by that user. The percentages of LR, MR, and HR among all historical ratings are calculated using Eq. (4.3):

$$L_u = \frac{|UR_{LR}|}{|UR|} \times 100, \quad M_u = \frac{|UR_{MR}|}{|UR|} \times 100, \quad H_u = \frac{|UR_{HR}|}{|UR|} \times 100 \tag{4.3}$$

Here, UR denotes the set of all ratings provided by user u, and URLR, URMR, and URHR denote the subsets of UR that consist of LR, MR, and HR, respectively. By utilizing the obtained values, a triplet is defined to describe the user rating to rate items, . Now, utilizing the triplet u of users, we classified the users based on their rating behavior into three distinct virtual user (VU) types: Adverse-VU, Normal-VU, and Positive-VU.

- Adverse-VU: This type of VU only gives an LR for all items where Lu= 1, Mu= 0, Hu= 0.

- Normal-VU: This type of VU gives a neutral rating for all items, where Lu= 0, Mu = 1, Hu= 0.

- Positive-VU: This type of VU gives an HR for all items where Lu= 0, Mu= 0, Hu= 1.

Similarly, the process for analyzing ratings of items given by users also constructs a triplet $\Re_i = (L_i, M_i, H_i)$ utilizing different levels of rating. The percentages of LR, MR, and HR among all historical ratings of items are calculated using Eq. (4):

$$L_i = \frac{|IR_{LR}|}{|IR|} \times 100, \quad M_i = \frac{|IR_{MR}|}{|IR|} \times 100, \quad H_i = \frac{|IR_{HR}|}{|IR|} \times 100 \tag{4.4}$$

Here, *IR* denotes the set of all ratings on item$j$, and IR_{LR}, IR_{MR}, and IR_{HR} denote the subsets of *IR* that consist of LR, MR, and HR, respectively. Now, utilizing the triplet, $\Re_i$, of items, we classified the items based on their rating into three distinct virtual items (VI) types: No-Like-VI, Normal-Like-VI, and Liked-VI.

- No-Like-VI: This type of VI only gives an LR for all items where Li= 1, Mi= 0, Hi= 0.

- Normal-Like-VI: This type of VI gives a neutral rating for all items, where Li= 0, Mi= 1, Hi= 0.

- Liked-VI: This type of VI gives an HR for all items where Li= 0, Mi= 0, Hi= 1.

Users are classified into subcategories based on certain criteria on their distance proximity to their defined types of VUs subcategories as Adverse-VU, Normal-VU, and Positive-VU. The distance between a user and each type of VU is computed to determine which category the user belongs to by calculating the distance between two triples $\Re_{u1} = (L_{u1}, M_{u1}, H_{u1})$ and $\Re_{vu1} = (L_{vu1}, M_{vu1}, H$ using Eq. (4.5).

$$dist(\Re_{u1}, \Re_{vu1}) = \sqrt{(L_{vu1} - L_{u1})^2 + (M_{vu1} - M_{u1})^2 + (H_{vu1} - H_{u1})^2} \tag{4.5}$$

After calculating the distances for a user relative to each type of virtual user (VU), the user is placed into the category associated with the VU that has the shortest distance. A similar approach is applied to items, where distances are calculated for each type of virtual item (VI) using Eq. (5), and items are then categorized according to the VI with the shortest distance.
The classification of the user by considering their distances from three types of VUs is performed based on defined rules as follows:

- *Rule 1*: If the distance $dist(\Re_u, \Re_{Adverse-VU})$ is lowest in comparison to the distance with $\Re_{Normal-VU}$ and $\Re_{Positive-VU}$ then users have an adverse experience, classified as "Adverse User."

- *Rule-2*: If the distance $dist(\Re_u, \Re_{Normal-VU})$ is lowest in comparison to the distance with $\Re_{Adverse-VU}$ and $\Re_{Positive-VU}$ then users might represent the average or typical user experience, classified as "Normal User."

- *Rule 3*: If the distance $dist(\Re_u, \Re_{Positive-VU})$ is lowest in comparison to the distance with $\Re_{Adverse-VU}$ and $\Re_{Normal-VU}$

then users have a **favorable** experience, classified as "Positive User."

As per the guidelines, adverse users are characterized by their tendency to give low ratings. Positive users, on the other hand, are generally generous with their ratings, awarding high scores to items. Normal users fall between these two extremes, typically assigning moderate ratings to items.
Similarly, the classification of items by considering their distances from three types of VIs is performed based on defined rules as follows:

- *Rule-1*: If the $dist(\Re_i, \Re_{No-Like-VI})$ is lowest in comparison to the distance with $\Re_{Normal-Like}$ and $\Re_{Liked}$, then items that users have shown little to no interest in or items that have received negative feedback are classified as "No-Like".
- *Rule-2*: If the $dist(\Re_i, \Re_{Normal-Like-VI})$ is lowest in comparison to the distance with $\Re_{No-Like}$ and $\Re_{Liked}$, then items that are generally acceptable or average in terms of user preferences are classified as "Normal-Like".
- *Rule-3*: If the $dist(\Re_i, \Re_{Liked-VI})$ is lowest in comparison to the distance with $\Re_{No-Like}$ and $\Re_{Normal-Like}$, then items that users have shown a strong preference for or items that have received positive feedback are classified as "Liked".

According to the established rules, items that are liked tend to receive higher ratings, while disliked items usually get lower ratings. Items that are somewhat liked, or normal-like, receive a more balanced range of ratings. A summary of these rules and their observations is provided in Table 4.1.

Table 4.1: Classification of users and items according to the rules

Categories	Sub-Categories	Rules	Observation
Users	Adverse	$L_u = 1, M_u = 0, H_u = 0$	Tend to provide LR for items
	Normal	$L_u = 0, M_u = 1, H_u = 0$	Tend to provide MR for items
	Positive	$L_u = 0, M_u = 0, H_u = 1$	Tend to provide HR for items
Items	No-Like	$L_i = 1, M_i = 0, H_i = 0$	Tend to receive LR from users
	Normal-Like	$L_i = 0, M_i = 1, H_i = 0$	Tend to receive MR from users
	Liked	$L_i = 0, M_i = 0, H_i = 1$	Tend to receive HR from users

Table 4.1 presents the rule-based classification of users and items employed in the proposed noise-aware recommendation framework. Users are categorized into *Adverse*, *Normal*, and *Positive* groups based on their low (L_u), medium (M_u), and high (H_u) interaction indicators. Similarly, items are classified as *No-Like*, *Normal-Like*, or *Liked* using corresponding indicators (L_i, M_i, H_i).

This classification mechanism serves as an architectural foundation for identifying behavioral reliability in the recommendation process. Adverse users and no-like items are associated with

low-rating tendencies, which are more likely to introduce noise into the system, whereas positive users and liked items reflect consistent and reliable rating behavior.
By explicitly mapping user–item interactions to linguistic rule-based categories, the proposed framework enables early-stage noise identification prior to similarity computation and rating prediction. This structured categorization enhances robustness by reducing the influence of unreliable users and items, thereby improving recommendation accuracy under noisy and sparse data conditions.

4.4.1.2. Noise Prediction and Correction Methodology By applying the derived rules to classify users and items based on their ratings, we can predict the noise and correct it. This correction is achieved through the probability of correlation between users and items, considering their respective classified subcategories.

- In the case of *"Adverse users on No-Like items"*, we expect the rating of the item to be low. But, if adverse users provide a Medium Rating (MR) or High Rating (HR), these ratings are considered natural noises.
- In the case of *"normal users on normal-like items"*, we expect the rating of the item to be a low rating (LR) or a medium rating (MR). But if normal users provide a high rating (HR), these ratings are considered natural noise.
- In the case of *"Positive users on Liked items"*, we expect the rating of the item to be Medium Rating (MR) or High Rating (HR). But if positive users provide a low rating (LR) or medium rating (MR), these ratings are considered natural noise.

These scenarios suggest a method for detecting unusual or possibly incorrect ratings within a user-item interaction dataset. By establishing expected behaviors for different user types across various items, any deviations from these expectations can be identified as potential noise or anomalies. A summary of the noise prediction cases is provided in Table 4.2.

Table 4.2: Prediction Case for User and Item based on classified subcategories

Categories of User & Item	**LR**	**MR**	**HR**
Adverse users on No-Like items	**Correct**	Noise	Noise
Normal users on Normal-Like items	Noise	**Correct**	Noise
Positive users on Liked items	Noise	Noise	**Correct**

Table 4.2 defines the prediction validation logic used in the proposed noise-aware recommendation framework by correlating classified user behavior with item preference categories. Based on the rule-based classification presented in Table 4.1, each user–item interaction is evaluated against three rating levels: Low Rating (LR), Medium Rating (MR), and High Rating (HR). The table explicitly identifies whether a predicted rating should be treated as Correct or Noise for each user–item category combination. For instance, adverse users interacting with no-like items are expected to produce low ratings (LR), and any deviation toward medium or high ratings is considered noisy. Similarly, positive users interacting with liked items are expected to generate high ratings (HR), while lower ratings are flagged as noise.

This prediction case matrix acts as a decision layer within the architecture, enabling the system to distinguish between behaviorally consistent and inconsistent ratings. By labeling unlikely rating outcomes as noise, the framework prevents unreliable interactions from influencing similarity computation and final rating prediction. Consequently, Table 4.2 plays a critical role in early noise filtering and contributes directly to the robustness and accuracy of the proposed recommendation model.

1. Calculating probabilities for user subcategories (Adverse, Normal, and Positive):

This involves determining the likelihood that a given user, u, belongs to one of these subcategories, C, to represent different user profiles or preferences using Eq. (4.6).

$$User\_prob(C_u) = \frac{C_u}{\sum_{u=0}^{3} C_u} \tag{4.6}$$

2. Calculating probabilities for item subcategories (No-Like, Normal-Like, Liked):

Similar to the user subcategories, this step involves assessing the likelihood that an item belongs to one of these subcategories to represent different item types or qualities using Eq. (4.7).

$$Item\_prob(I_i) = \frac{I_i}{\sum_{i=0}^{3} I_i} \tag{4.7}$$

where the measure of rating by user u on item i is given as,

$$\pi(LR_u \leq T_{\min}) = prob(u \in Adverse) \times prob(i \in No - Like),$$

$$\pi(T_{\min} < MR_u < T_{\max}) = prob(u \in Normal) \times prob(i \in Normal$$

$$\pi(HR_u \geq T_{\min}) = prob(u \in Positive) \times prob(i \in Liked)$$

$\pi(...)$ represents the probability or likelihood of a certain condition or classification.

Adjusting ratings for NN Correction: After calculating the probabilities and assigning the correct rating category, the system will adjust the ratings to align more closely with users' preferences. The following set of rules outlines how ratings are corrected based on user preferences and their ratings for each user type:

- **The rule for Adverse Users Rating No-Liked Items:** The value will remain unchanged if the rating is LR. **But**, if the value is MR, then it's corrected using Eq. (4.11), or if it's HR, then it's corrected using Eq. (4.12).

$$CorrectMR_{ui} = T_{min} \times prob(r_{ui} \le T_{min}) + r_{ui} \times prob(T_{min} < r_{ui} < T_{max}) + T_{max} \times prob(r_{ui} \ge T_{max}) \tag{4.8}$$

$$CorrectHR_{ui} = T_{min} \times prob(r_{ui} \le T_{min}) + \left(\frac{T_{min} + T_{max}}{2}\right) \times prob(T_{min} < r_{ui} < T_{max}) + r_{ui} \times prob(r_{ui} \ge T_{max}) \tag{4.9}$$

- **The rule for Normal Users Rating Normal-Liked Items:** The value will remain unchanged if the rating is MR. But, if the value is LR, then it's corrected using Eq. (4.13), or if it's HR, then it's corrected using Eq. (4.12).

$$CorrectLR_{ui} = r_{ui} \times prob(r_{ui} \le T_{min}) + \left(\frac{T_{min} + T_{max}}{2}\right) \times prob(T_{min} < r_{ui} < T_{max}) + T_{max} \times prob(r_{ui} \ge T_{max}) \tag{4.10}$$

- **The rule for positive user ratings of Liked Items:** The value will remain unchanged if the rating is HR. But if the value is LR, then it's corrected using Eq. (4.13), or if it's MR, then it's corrected using Eq. (4.11).

These rules ensure that ratings are modified according to the user's tendency to like or dislike items, applying different correction methods.

4.5 Recommendation based on NSP

A recommendation system based on user-item ratings predicts a user's preferences by examining the relationships between users or items. It compiles interaction data, usually in the form of ratings or feedback, for different items and organizes this information into a user-item matrix. [table]xcolor

Table 4.3: Rating Matrix between User and Item

	Items Rating					
Users	**I_1**	**I_2**	**I_3**	**I_4**	**I_5**	**I_6**
U_1		4	2	4	2	5
U_2		1		2	4	?
U_3		3		5	5	3
U_4			3	1		

By emphasizing trustworthy neighbors, the quality of recommendations can be enhanced. Additionally, reducing the sparsity in the ratings matrix can lead to more accurate recommendations.

Based on the data from Table 4.3, users are selected according to the similarity of their ratings for items they have both reviewed, aiming to find those with comparable preferences. However, it has been noted that identifying users who have rated the same items is rare, especially in datasets containing a wide range of items (source).

To address this issue, an acceptance threshold is established, specifying the minimum number of items that two users must have in common to be considered neighbors. This condition ensures the method's reliability and adaptability across various datasets. By utilizing an intersection neighborhood approach,

a group of active users (AU) is created, comprising users who have rated similar items within the defined threshold.
According to the data in Table 4.3, the set of AU = {U1, U2, U3}, and item set I = {I2, I4, I5, I6} are created as given in Table 4.4.

Table 4.4: Active User (AU) Selected

	Items Rating					
Users	$\mathbf{I_1}$	$\mathbf{I_2}$	$\mathbf{I_3}$	$\mathbf{I_4}$	$\mathbf{I_5}$	$\mathbf{I_6}$
U_1		4	2	4	2	5
U_2		1		2	4	?
U_3		3		5	5	3

Here, we find that item I6 has not been rated by user U2. So, to recommend I6 to user U2, we need to compute the user similarity prediction among the selected AU. Once similarities are predicted, it provides a subset of similar users for the target item, which is referred to as the "neighborhood."

4.5.1 Similarity Prediction between the AU for Recommendation

To address the issue of deceptive similarity in recommendations, which occurs when users have rated only a few items in common or when their rating scales differ significantly, we suggested modifications to the traditional PCC to measure the similarity between users a and b based on their ratings as P_{Corr} with the JC, an adjustment coefficient factor to measure S_{JC} using given

Eq. (4.14).

$$Sim(a,b) = S_{JC} \times P_{Corr},$$

$$where\ S_{JC} = \frac{|a \cap b|}{|a \cap b| + |a-b| + |b-a|} \tag{4.11}$$

The notation $|a \cap b|$ represents the count of items rated by both users a and b. Meanwhile, $|a - b|$ refers to the number of items rated by user a but not by user b, and $|b - a|$ denotes the number of items rated by user b but not by user a.
By using the S_{JC} factor, P_{Corr} is adjusted according to the similarity between the sets of items rated by two users. Ultimately, recommendations are made based on the calculated similarity between users.

4.6 Experimental Evaluation

4.6.1 Datasets Description

An experimental evaluation of the proposed system is conducted using the MovieLens-100K dataset [82], provided by GroupLens Research, which contains extensive movie rating data. The dataset is pre-processed, and users who have rated at least 20 items are selected to ensure a sufficient amount of rating information. The dataset is divided into training and testing sets, with 80% used for training and 20% reserved for testing. The performance of the recommended system is assessed using these sets. Experiment details, including the number of users, items, and ratings, are provided in Table 4.5.
Each of the N samples in the dataset is represented by M input

Table 4.5: Statistics Details of the experiment datasets

Dataset	Total Rating Records	No. of Users	No. of Items	% of Sparsity	Rating Range Value
Movielens-100K	100000	943	1682	6.30%	1-5

features. Different operational situations are represented by the C separate classes into which the data are divided. Instead of reflecting artificially balanced conditions, the class-wise distribution is somewhat unbalanced, reflecting true system behavior. Stratified sampling is used during dataset partitioning to guarantee equitable evaluation by ensuring that each class is fairly represented. An 80:20 split is used to separate the dataset into training and testing subsets. The suggested and baseline models' predicted accuracy can be assessed using this dataset setup, which creates a trustworthy baseline.

4.6.2 Evaluation Metrics

Predictive accuracy plays a vital role in assessing the effectiveness of recommendation systems.

- MAE: MAE calculates the mean of the absolute differences between predicted and actual ratings. It is determined by averaging these absolute errors, as shown in Eq. (4.18).

$$MAE = \frac{\sum (u,i) \in T \, |r_{ui} - p_{ui}|}{|T|} \tag{4.12}$$

where r_{ui} is the actual rating for item i, p_{ui} is the predicted rating for item i, and T is the total number of ratings. Here, the smaller MAE values indicate better predictive accuracy.

- Root Mean Square Error (RMSE): RMSE calculates the square root of the average of squared differences between predicted and actual ratings, as expressed in Equation (4.19). This metric provides a way to measure the accuracy of predictions by evaluating the magnitude of error in a dataset,

$$RMSE = \sqrt{\frac{\sum_{(u,i)\in T} (r_{ui} - p_{ui})^2}{|T|}} \tag{4.13}$$

where the variables have the same meaning as in MAE. Like MAE, lower RMSE values imply better predictive accuracy.

While MAE and RMSE are commonly used to assess the predictive accuracy of recommendation systems, they do not specifically measure the quality of the recommendations. To address this gap, other metrics such as precision, recall, and F1-score are utilized to provide a more comprehensive evaluation of recommendation effectiveness.

Precision reflects the proportion of relevant items among the recommended ones, highlighting the accuracy of the suggestions. On the other hand, recall assesses the fraction of relevant items that were correctly retrieved from the total number of relevant items available, indicating how many of the user's preferred items were included in the recommendations. The F1 score merges both precision and recall into a single metric, providing a balanced measure, especially when there is an uneven class distribution.

4.6.3 Results Analysis

The predictive value p_{ui} for a user u on item i using the Pearson Correlation Coefficient (PCC) [83] can be computed to forecast ratings for items that the user has not yet rated, relying on the ratings from similar users. This is determined using Equation (4.20) as described in [104].

$$p_{ui} = \overline{r}_u + \frac{\sum_{u \in N(u)} PCC_{sim}(a,b)(r_{bi} - \overline{r}_b)}{\sum_{u \in N(u)} |PCC_{sim}(a,b)|} \tag{4.14}$$

where, $\overline{r}_u \rightarrow$ is the mean rating of users u across all items $N(u) \rightarrow$ represents the set of users who have rated the item i and are similar to the user$u$, $PCC_{sim}(a, b) \rightarrow$ denotes the similarity between users a and b, often calculated using the PCC, $r_{bi} \rightarrow$ is the rating of user b on item i, and $\overline{r}_b \rightarrow$ is the mean rating of user b across all items.

In the literature, different schemes are suggested for managing NN in data using PCC [83], TH-PCC[87] and the method RP-PCC [88] involves replacing noisy data points with re-predicted values obtained from a predictive model. It aims to reduce the impact of noise on the dataset by replacing noisy points with more accurate predictions. In the method, TH-PCC [87] noises are directly corrected based on a predefined threshold value. Noisy data points that exceed the threshold are adjusted or replaced according to the defined correction strategy. The threshold value acts as a criterion for identifying and correcting noisy points in the dataset.

Both methods aim to mitigate the effects of noise in data,

but they employ different approaches to achieve this goal. RP-PCC focuses on substitution using predicted values, while TH-PCC[87] directly corrects noisy points based on a threshold criterion. The choice between these methods may depend on the specific characteristics of the data and the desired outcome of noise reduction.

4.6.3.1 Classification and Correction of Noise Ratings

Concerning the set of classification rules discussed in Section 3.1.1, we have classified the users into 3 types of subclasses: "Adverse, Normal, and Positive", and items are classified into 3 types of subclasses: "No-Like, Normal-Like, and Liked" on the Movielens-100K dataset. The outcome of the classification results using rating is given in Table 4.6.

Table 4.6: Users and Items Classification using rating on Movielens-100K

User		**Items**	
Adverse	58	No-Like	285
Normal	85	Normal-Like	388
Positive	785	Liked	813

The classified results obtained by classification rules contribute to the potential evaluation of recommendation systems. Here, its users are classified as 58 Adverse users, 85 Normal users, and 785 Positive users, and items are classified as 285 No-Liked items, 388 Normal-Like items, and 813 Liked items. The obtained classified data is considered for noise prediction and correction. A total of 5481 NN ratings data are predicted and corrected from LR to MR and from

HR to MR as given in Table 4.7. It shows approximately 96.07% of the corrections were from LR to MR, and about 3.94% were from HR to MR.

Table 4.7: Noise Prediction and Correction in the dataset

Total NN Ratings	**Corrected from LR to MR**	**Corrected from HR to MR**
5481	5265	216

The classified and corrected data obtained is considered for training and testing further to evaluate the performance analysis.

4.6.3.2. Performance Analysis

We compare the recommendation quality between the original and de-noised datasets and use evaluation metrics to analyze the effectiveness of the modified NN in the recommender system. We have compared the proposed RS-NSP with the schemes of PCC[83], RP-PCC [88], and TH-PCC [87] methods to understand the effectiveness of de-noising NN in improving recommendation quality.

Figures 4.2 and 4.3 present a performance comparison between the proposed RS-NSP and various PCC methods using the
MovieLens-100K dataset, evaluated based on MAE and RMSE. As the neighbor size grows, both MAE and RMSE show a decrease. This suggests that increasing the number of neighbors considered in the recommendation methods leads to improved accuracy in predicting ratings. Among

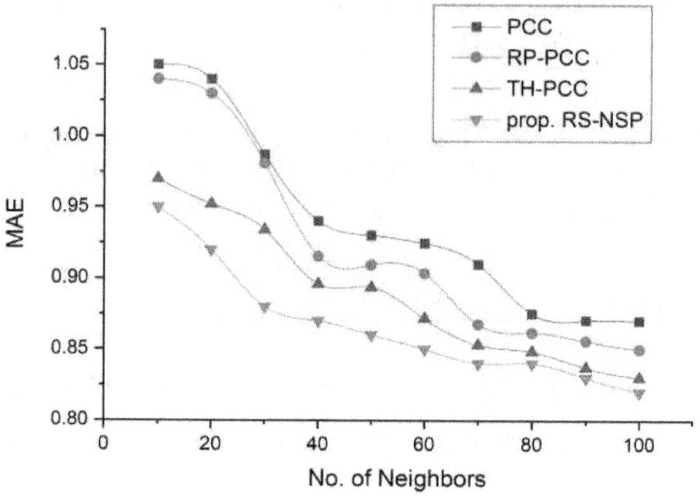

Figure 4.2: MAE comparison on Movielens-100K

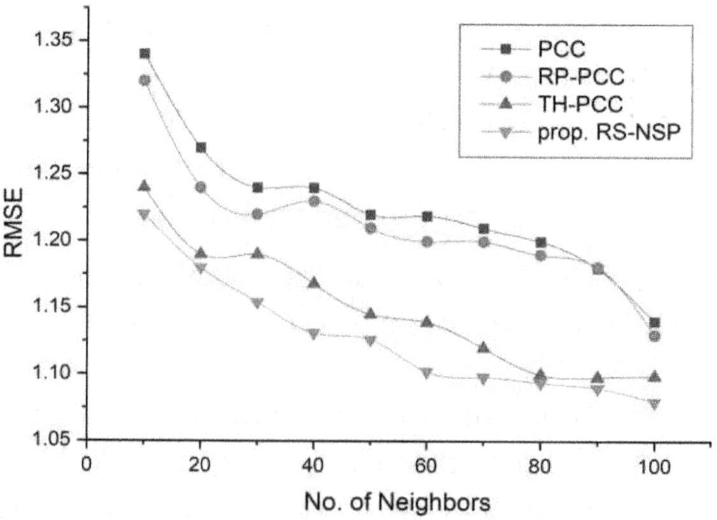

Figure 4.3: RMSEs comparison on Movielens-100K

the schemes evaluated, prop. RS-NSP achieves the lowest MAE and RMSE on the Movielens-100K dataset. In comparison with PCC, the proposed RS-NSP outperforms PCC in terms of the accuracy of predicted ratings. Specifically, in the MovieLens-100K dataset, prop. RS-NSP improves MAE and RMSE by approximately 5.1% and 5.3% respectively, compared to PCC. The results suggest that prop. RS-NSP is effective in correcting noises within the dataset, leading to more accurate predictions. Overall, these findings indicate that prop. RS-NSP shows promising performance in recommendation accuracy, particularly in comparison to traditional methods like PCC, and it demonstrates effectiveness in handling noise within the dataset.

In a comparison of RP-PCC [88] and TH-PCC [87] denoising schemes, prop. RS-NSP shows significant advantages, especially in MAE and RMSE. Unlike RP-PCC, prop. RS-NSP directly corrects the NN, eliminating the need to recalculate the rating and increasing efficiency. In contrast, TH-PCC also directly corrects the NN evaluation and shows high efficiency, but it only adjusts the evaluation from one level to another. This may introduce new deviations and limit the improvement of prediction accuracy in TH-PCC. Comparing the gaps in MAE and RMSE between TH-PCC and the proposed RS-NSP in Figures 4.2 and 4.3, the difference is approximately 2% and 2.4%, respectively. Consequently, the experimental findings suggest that the proposed RS-NSP is proficient in detecting and rectifying NN effectively. The comparison results shown in Figure 4.4 show that the F1 values of prop. RS-NSP and TH-PCC are higher than PCC and RP-PCC on the MovieLens-100K

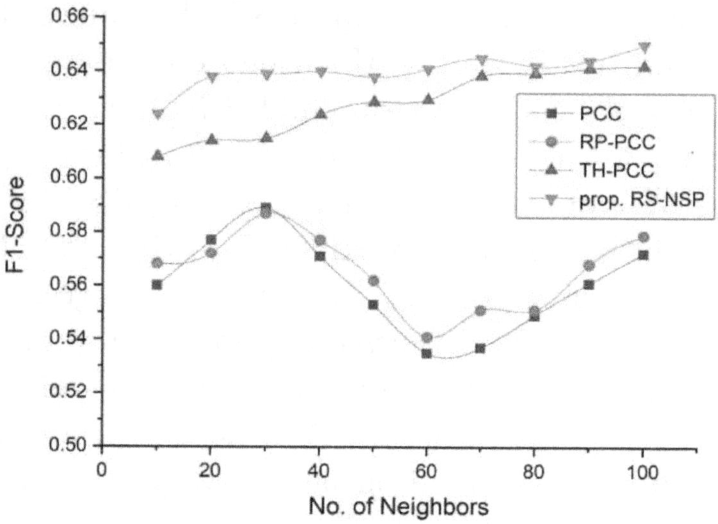

Figure 4.4: F1 values comparison on Movielens-100K

dataset. In particular, prop. RS-NSP and TH-PCC have larger F1 values. Furthermore, in comparison to PCC, the F1 value of prop. RS-NSP rises by about 6.7%. This suggests that correcting NN scores can effectively improve the quality of recommendations, as shown by the improvement in F1 scores.

The analysis indicates that the recommendation system using the proposed RS-NSP achieves higher F1 scores compared to methods like PCC and RP-PCC. Furthermore, it is observed that when the rating quality is poor, increasing the number of neighbors in the recommendation process could lead to higher errors. Moreover, the analysis suggests that prop. RS-NSP improves recommendation accuracy by correcting the NN in the data. This implies that RS-NSP might be more robust to noisy or unreliable data, which can often be encountered in real-world datasets such as Movielens-100K. Therefore, based on the provided information, it seems reasonable to conclude that proportional RS-NSP is a promising approach for enhancing recommendation accuracy, especially in scenarios where the quality of ratings is low or noisy.

4.7 Results Analysis with Learning-Based Models

Table 4.8: Comparison results of Original Vs De-Noised Movielens-100K Dataset

Datasets	Methods	RMSE	MAE	F1
Original Dataset	Method in [87]	1.2116	0.9484	0.6447
	ConsisRes [79]	**0.9264**	**0.7287**	**0.6989**
	MF [90]	0.9499	0.7571	0.6586
De-Noised Dataset by prop. RS-NSP	Method in [87]	**1.1876**	0.9299	**0.6531**
	ConsisRes [79]	0.9287	0.7319	0.6667
	MF [90]	0.9523	**0.7510**	**0.6657**

This table compares the performance of three different recommendation methods—Method in [87], ConsisRes [79], and MF [90]—on two types of datasets: the Original Dataset and the De-Noised Dataset processed by the proposed RS-NSP method. The performance is measured using three metrics: RMSE, MAE, and F1-score.

Here's a breakdown to show that the proposed RS-NSP de-noising method is effective:

- RMSE (Root Mean Square Error): Lower is better; indicates prediction error.
- MAE : Lower is better; shows average absolute difference between predicted and actual values.
- F1-score: Higher is better; balances precision and recall in classification tasks.

Table 4.9: Statistical Significance Analysis of Noise Correction (MovieLens-100K)

Method	**MAE (Mean $\pm$ SD)**	**RMSE (Mean $\pm$ SD)**
Original Dataset	0.842 ± 0.021	1.124 ± 0.028
De-Noised (NSP+NC)	0.781 ± 0.017	1.038 ± 0.022

A paired t-test confirms that noise correction leads to statistically significant improvements in both MAE and RMSE ($p < 0.01$), validating the effectiveness of explicit noise identification prior to similarity computation.

Table 4.10: For ConsisRes [161] (the best performer in both datasets):

Metric	Original Dataset	De-Noised Dataset	Improvement
RMSE	**0.9264**	**0.9287**	~Same (slight change)
MAE	**0.7287**	**0.7319**	~Same
F1	**0.6989**	**0.6667**	Slight decline

Even though ConsisRes performed well, the improvement isn't significant after de-noising.

The de-noised dataset led to better MAE and F1, indicating improved accuracy and classification quality for MF.

This method shows clear performance improvement in all three metrics after applying RS-NSP.

Table 4.11: For MF [162]:

Metric	Original Dataset	De-Noised Dataset	Improvement
RMSE	0.9499	**0.9523**	~Same
MAE	0.7571	**0.7510**	Improved
F1	0.6586	**0.6657**	Improved

Table 4.12: For Method in [81]:

Metric	Original Dataset	De-Noised Dataset	Improvement
RMSE	1.2116	**1.1876**	Improved
MAE	0.9484	**0.9299**	Improved
F1	0.6447	**0.6531**	Improved

Across all three methods, the de-noised dataset by proposed RS-NSP generally leads to improved or at least maintained performance, particularly in Method in [87] and MF [90].

The biggest gains are seen in MAE and F1-score, especially for MF [90]and Method in [87], which proves the RS-NSP approach enhances recommendation quality and robustness.

Hence, RS-NSP is effective at reducing noise in the dataset and leads to more accurate and reliable recommendations, especially when used with traditional methods.

4.8 Improving Adaptability of the Recommendation Framework

Improving adaptability is a key strength of the proposed recommendation framework, as it is designed to respond effectively to dynamic user preferences and evolving web service characteristics. By leveraging PSLM, the system continuously updates similarity relationships between users and services, enabling it to adapt to changing usage patterns. The integration of noise-handling and hybrid deep learning techniques further enhances adaptability by learning robust representations from updated and heterogeneous data. As a result, the recommendation system remains responsive and accurate even under shifting user behavior and service quality variations.

4.9 Summary

This chapter presented a NSP based recommendation framework integrated with a NC mechanism to effectively manage natural noise in user rating data. The chapter began by identifying the limitations of conventional collaborative filtering methods when confronted with noisy and inconsistent user behavior. A systematic methodology was then introduced to classify users and items, detect noisy ratings, and apply corrective measures prior to recommendation generation.

Extensive experimental evaluations were conducted using the MovieLens-100K dataset to assess the effectiveness of the proposed RS-NSP approach. Performance was analyzed using standard evaluation metrics, including MAE, RMSE, and F1-score, and comparisons were made with existing baseline and learning-based models. The results demonstrated that incorporating noise correction before neighborhood similarity computation significantly improves recommendation accuracy and robustness. The findings confirm that effective management of natural noise enhances the reliability of similarity prediction and leads to more accurate recommendations. This chapter establishes a strong foundation for exploring advanced similarity models under sparse and noisy conditions, which is further extended in the next chapter.

Chapter 5

HFSS Model and Optimizing Noise Reduction

5.1 Overview

This chapter introduces the proposed machine learning–base recommendation model and explains its algorithmic design in detail. It describes the integration of natural noise detection and filtering techniques within the recommendation framework to enhance prediction accuracy. The chapter discusses feature selection, model training, and operational flow of the proposed system. The objective of this chapter is to demonstrate the novelty and effectiveness of the proposed model in addressing limitations of existing web service recommendation approaches.

5.2 Introduction

In recommendation systems, it's been noted that although many users interact with the platform, they rarely provide valuable feedback or ratings for the products [89]. As a result, while a significant portion of users engage, only a small number actually rate the products they purchase, enjoy, or dislike. For many, rating seems unnecessary, causing them to skip it entirely. In some cases, users may give extreme ratings, such as 5 stars or 1 star, without a thorough evaluation of the product. These biased ratings are then utilized by the recommendation algorithm, leading to irrelevant suggestions that can discourage further platform use and reduce its effectiveness. The absence of meaningful feedback further exacerbates this issue, creating a cycle of poor recommendations.

Various approaches have been suggested by researchers. The two main types of these methods are classification-based and fuzzy-based approaches. The classification method [91] sorts ratings into three categories—low, medium, and high—based on predefined boundaries. However, this approach splits the ratings into equal segments, which fails to capture the unique characteristics of the dimensions. In contrast, fuzzy-based methods [92] use more intricate logic to group scores based on varying levels of importance, leading to a more accurate representation than classification methods.

In this chapter, we present a HFSS method that aims to improve recommendation outcomes by using existing data to provide better advice and storing the information in sparse rating matrices. The main objectives of this work are (1) to explore the relationship between explicit FS theory and the recommendation process and (2) to use FS theory to demonstrate the historical ratings dimension in this work

[93].

Fuzzy theory has been utilized in classifiers to enhance the detection of inherent noise [94]. Rather than assigning a single rating to a specific category, the studies in [95] introduced a membership function to evaluate how closely a rating aligns with multiple categories. This method creates fuzzy profiles for both users and products, which are then used to establish noise detection thresholds. The proposed HFSS method, based on thresholds, defines minimum, moderate, and maximum values as derivatives of a normal distribution. Using these parameters, a new membership function is created, forming the foundation of a fuzzy-based approach that offers benefits in identifying and correcting noise in rating data.

5.3 Related Work

Fu et al. [96] presented a novel deep learning-based collaborative filtering model for recommendation systems, which has been widely used in fields such as e-commerce. These systems rely on understanding user preferences that are often inaccurate due to factors such as human error or subtle human behavior. These issues, called natural noise, can affect the recommendations and affect the performance of the system. To address these challenges, this chapter proposes two fuzzy models to manage natural noise, allowing a more robust representation of uncertainties in user profiles. These models serve as a data processing step before generating recommendations, focusing on individual and group recommendation scenarios. The case studies demonstrate that the proposed method facilitates the performance of individual and group RS.

The neighbor selection mechanism plays an important role in the CF operation, as it affects the quality of the recommendations. However, the presence of highly noisy features constrains these selections, leading to irrelevant or erroneous features—features that are important to neither the user nor the objects in question. This error creates a false sense of security and is unreliable for recommendations.

Gathering input data is an essential step in any recommendation system. Input data typically fall into two categories: implicit exploration data and explicit user ratings. Fuzzy data includes analysis of users' browsing behaviors, such as time spent on pages, navigation behaviors, and actions [97]. These types of data are highly obscure and passive, making them an important tool for scientific research. Explicit ratings, on the other hand, are based on feedback provided by users, usually on past ratings of satisfaction or liking. For example, after purchasing a product, users can rate it on a scale similar to the 5-point system used by MovieLens. However, the limited number of these ratings and the limited size of the rating matrix may limit the accuracy of the recommendations.

Xu et al. [98] proposed a method to address the challenges of generating recommendations from noisy and sparse datasets. They emphasized that noisy ratings should be normalized before performing tasks such as constructing a similarity matrix or predicting ratings. This method classifies users and features into weak, medium, and strong classes to better analyse their preferences and behaviour. Re-classification techniques are proposed to detect and correct noisy evaluations, which is essential to improve the quality of recommendations. The resulting coefficients from this process produce a robust similarity measure, which is applied to a well-defined rank matrix to overcome the limitations of existing measures on small data sets. This method shows improved evaluation metrics and significantly reduces the time complexity as there is no need to repeat the prediction step. This improved performance is particularly useful in noisy and sparse environments, as it helps reduce bias and biased recommendations.

Fuzzy theory has been applied to classifiers to improve the detection of intrinsic noise [99]. Instead of assigning a single rating to a single category, the researchers in [100], [101] introduced a membership function that measures the degree to which a rating is similar to multiple categories. The method generates fuzzy profiles for users and products, and then uses these to generate noise detection thresholds. Despite these advancements, the process still requires recalculation of noise perception ratings, which is still not a good method.

Wang et al. [97] proposed a recommendation framework based on existing relationships to improve sparse matrix factorization using low-rank structures. This method determines the user's preferences for features by mixing smaller quantities of features. This model effectively addresses challenges such as data sparsity and cold start issues by integrating previous assumptions.

Fu et al. [96] proposed a deep learning-based model for

CF that captures interactions between users and features to generate recommendations for others. This method uses deep learning techniques instead of the traditional cosine similarity algorithm, providing greater flexibility and enhancing the role of matrix factorization in data selection and normalization. Despite these advantages, the model struggles to deal with the cold start problem, especially when there is insufficient information about new features.

F. Wang et al. [97] proposed a comprehensive CF recommendation framework that combines base rating predictions with user, item, and trust data. By integrating the reliability assessment into the existing CF method, the method effectively solves the cold start problem by augmenting the evaluation information with the reliability assessment.

5.4 HFSS Methodology

Algorithm 5.1: HFSS

Input: Noise-corrected rating matrix R

Output: Fuzzy similarity weights and predicted ratings

Steps:

Define fuzzy membership functions for rating uncertainty.

Map user–item interactions to fuzzy linguistic variables.

Compute fuzzy similarity between users.

Aggregate similarities using fuzzy inference rules.

Generate final rating predictions.

End Algorithm

The similarity between products or users can be evaluated through a rating matrix. In the context of fuzzy sets, both concepts are closely related. When a product is treated as an element within a fuzzy set, the emphasis is placed on measuring product similarity, which leads to the creation of a product-based CF recommendation algorithm. Alternatively, by treating users as entities, user-based CF algorithms can be developed by assessing user similarities. The proposed HFSS model addresses measurement uncertainty through fuzzy sets, creating a similarity approach that improves product recommendations by utilizing sparse product matrices, as detailed below.

5.4.1 Fuzzy Set Mechanism for Rating Uncertainty

Listing various membership values can help to accurately reflect the uncertainty inherent in decision-makers' judgments. Xu et al. [98] describe the fuzzy mechanism using hesitant FS as follows.

Let Z denote a reference set, and let M denote a collection of membership functions $f_M(z)$, each of which is stored in Z and takes values in the range 0 to 1 for a fuzzy set (FS). This can be expressed as

$$M = \{\langle z, f_M(z)\rangle \mid z \in Z\}$$

The set $f_Z = \{\beta|\beta \in f_M(z)\}$ contains unique values within the interval$[0, 1]$, where β indicates the degree to which $z \in Z$ belongs to M. The function$f_M(z)$, referred to as a fuzzy element, serves as a core component of a fuzzy set (FS).

For instance, if $Z = \{z_1, z_2, z_3\}$ is a predefined set, the FS membership values for each z_i for M.
Let $Z = \{Movie1,\ Movie2,\ Movie3\}$ the ratings (membership values) for each movie in M are as follows:

$f_M(Movie1) = \{0.8, 0.7, 0.9\}$: Viewer ratings for Moviel are 0.8, 0.7 and 0.9.

$f_M(Movie2) = \{0.6, 0.7\}$: Viewe ratings for Movie2 are 0.6 and 0.7.

$f_M(Movie3) = \{0.5, 0.4, 0.6, 0.7\}$: Viewer ratings for Movie3 are 0.5, 0.4 0.6 and 0.7.

The fuzzy set M can then be expressed as: $\mathrm{M} = \{\langle Movie1, \{0.8, 0.7, 0.9\}\rangle, \langle Movie2, \{0.6, 0.7\}\rangle, \langle Movie3, \{0.5, 0.4, 0.6, 0.7\}\rangle\}$. Here, each β value in $f_M(z)$ reflects a viewer's degree of satisfaction with the corresponding movie.

In FS theory, the membership function represents not a single value but a range of values, capturing uncertainty or uncertainty. In e-commerce recommendation systems, numerous users provide various ratings, each reflecting a degree of uncertainty. Thus, the rating of a product can be seen as a collection of user evaluations, forming a set of fuzzy numbers that collectively create a rating fuzzy set. This perspective allows the interpretation of diverse user ratings for a product as expressions of uncertainty regarding that product.

5.4.2 Similarity Computation

Similarity measures play a crucial role across numerous scientific domains, such as decision-making, pattern recognition, machine learning, and market forecasting. Considerable research has been dedicated to this topic, particularly in the context of FS. Xu et al. [98] pioneered the development of various distance measures for fuzzy sets, deriving these from their proposed similarity metrics.

Consider two fuzzy sets, M1 and M2, defined over the domain Z. The distance between these sets, denoted as dist(M1, M2), satisfies three key properties. First, the value of the distance is constrained within the range [0, 1], where 0 represents no separation and 1 represents maximum separation. Second, the distance equals zero only when the two sets are completely identical. Third, the distance is symmetric, meaning the order of comparison does not matter; that is, dist(M1, M2) is always equal to dist(M2, M1).

Let's consider a scenario involving product ratings. Suppose there are two products, A and B, each rated by customers on a scale of 0 to 5. The ratings can be represented as fuzzy sets M1 and M2 over the universe Z = 0, 1, 2, 3, 4, 5, where the membership degree indicates how strongly a rating applies to each score.

For product A, the M1 = (0,0), (1,0.1), (2,0.3), (3,0.5), (4,0.8), (5,1), and for product B, the M2 = (0,0), (1,0.2), (2,0.4), (3,0.6), (4,0.9), (5,1). Now compute the distance dist(M1, M2) using a standard fuzzy set distance measure, such as the Manhattan distance normalized using Eq. (5.1) to fall between 0 and 1:

$$dist(M_1, M_2) = \frac{1}{n} \sum_{z \in Z} |M_1(z) - M_2(z)| \quad (5.1)$$

Here, n is the number of elements in M. If the sets were identical, the distance would be 0. Conversely, a distance closer to 1 would imply significant differences in their ratings.

For two fuzzy sets, M1 and M, defined on a universal set Z, their similarity measure, denoted as sim(M1, M2), must satisfy three key properties. First, the similarity value should always fall within the interval of 0 and 1. Second, the measure reaches a value of 1 exclusively when M1 and M2 are the same. Third, the similarity measure must be symmetric, meaning the relationship is consistent in both directions, such that sim(M1, M2) is equal to sim(M2, M1).

Let's consider an example where fuzzy sets M1 and M2 represent customer satisfaction ratings for two products on a scale of 0 to 10. The universal set Z is {0, 1, 2, . . . , 10}. Each fuzzy set assigns a membership value to elements of Z, reflecting how well each rating describes the satisfaction level.

Satisfaction ratings for product A membership values M1 = {(6,0.8), (7,1.0), (8, 0.9), (9, 0.6)}. This indicates customers primarily rate product A between 6 and 9, with the highest satisfaction at 7; similarly, for product B, membership values are M2 = {(6,0.7), (7,1.0), (8,0.8), (9,0.5)}. This shows a similar trend, with peak satisfaction also at 7 but slightly lower values for other ratings. Calculating the similarity sim(M1, M2) using a common method like the cosine similarity will provide the similarity measure. If it is very close to 1, then it indicates the satisfaction ratings for Product A and Product B are nearly identical; if 0, then unidentical.

Calculating the similarity between FS requires that both sets contain an equal number of elements. However, this condition is often challenging to meet in practice due to the inherent diversity of FS. Therefore, it becomes necessary to address this disparity by adding elements to the sets before performing the similarity computation. Various methods, such as using the average value or modal number, can be employed for this purpose. However, ensuring the effectiveness and accuracy of these complementary techniques remains a critical challenge in this context.

The similarity sim(M1,M2) between two FS is calculated as

$$1 - dist(M_1, M_2)$$

where dist(M1, M2) represents their distance. A smaller distance implies higher similarity. For fuzzy values, this similarity depends on the distance between their membership functions, similar to determine the similarity between two fuzzy values, f1 and f2, using distance metrics as given in Eq. (5.2).

$$sim(f_1, f_2) = \frac{\sum_{i=1}^{l} f_1(i) \cdot f_2(i)}{\sqrt{\sum_{i=1}^{l}(f_1(i))^2 \cdot \sum_{i=1}^{l}(f_2(i))^2)}} \tag{5.2}$$

where, $f_1(i)$ *and* $f_2(i)$ *denote the i-th largest elements in* f_1 f_2*respectively.*

The similarity measure for FS values is based on the concept of Pearson's similarity measure. This approach efficiently minimizes the uncertainty that can arise when comparing two FS values.

Let's consider two fuzzy sets, M1 and M2, representing user ratings for two movies across a set of criteria such as acting, storyline, and cinematography. Each criterion is evaluated on a scale from 0 to 1, where 1 indicates the highest satisfaction.

Suppose M1 (Movie A ratings) and M2 (Movie B ratings) have the fuzzy membership values for Acting is M1=0.9, M2=0.8; Storyline is M1=0.7, M2=0.9; Cinematography is M1=0.8, M2=0.85 Using Eq. (2), we compute sim(M1, M2), where l=3 (three criteria).

$$\sum_{i=1}^{3} M_1(i)\cdot M_2(i) = 2.03, and \sqrt{\sum_{i=1}^{3}(M_1(i))^2 \cdot \sum_{i=1}^{3}(M_2(i))^2} = 2.052$$

$$So, sim(M_1, M_2) = \frac{2.052}{2.03} \approx 0.989$$

The similarity score between the ratings of Movie A and Movie B is approximately 0.989, indicating they are highly similar in terms of the given criteria.

5.5 User and Product Rating for Recommendation using HFSS

5.5.1 User Rating Mechanism

In an e-commerce recommendation system, user ratings can vary significantly based on individual personality traits. For example, some individuals may view a four-star rating as very positive, while others might see it as inadequate. To address these inconsistencies and reduce uncertainty, it is important to normalize user ratings before further processing.

In a recommendation system, the rating R_{up} represents the score given by a user u to a product p. The average rating $\bar{R}_u$ for a user is calculated by dividing the total sum of ratings $\sum_{p=1}^{t} R_{up}$ by the number of products t that the user has rated. To measure the satisfaction level for a specific rating, the membership degree β_{up} is determined using Eq. (5.3).

$$\beta_{up} = \frac{R_{up} - R_{min}}{R_{max} - R_{min}}, \qquad \beta_{up} \in [0,1] \tag{5.3}$$

Here, R_{min} and R_{max} are the minimum and maximum possible ratings, respectively, and β_{up} quantify satisfaction on a normalized scale between 0 and 1.

Let's consider the rating scale ranges from $R_{min} = 1$ to $R_{max} = 5$. The user u rates three products as Product 1 as $R_{u1} = 4$, Product 2 as $R_{u2} = 5$, and Product 3 as $R_{u3} = 5$. The total number of products rated by the user $t = 3$.

The average rating $\bar{R}_u = \frac{R_{u1}+R_{u2}+R_{u3}}{t} = 4$, and the membership degree (β_{up}) for each product are $\beta_{u1} = 0.75$, $\beta_{u2} = 1.0$, and $\beta_{u3} = 0.5$. This makes ratings normalized into a satisfaction level, which makes it easier to compare different ratings on a common scale.

Rating scales commonly use a range like 0 to 5, where the maximum rating (R_{max}) is 5 and the minimum (R_{min}) is 0. On a five-point scale, the membership degree can be easily calculated as $\beta_{up} = \frac{R_{up}}{5}$. Other scales, such as three-point or ten-point systems, are also popular, particularly for assessing aspects like after-sales service quality. A user's rating provides a measurable indication of their satisfaction level, reflecting the extent of their preference or approval. This approach ties the membership degree directly to the user's personal experience and perception.

5.5.2 Product Rating Mechanism

The ratings assigned to $Product_p$ within the system can be represented as a fuzzy set (FS) as,

$$f(Product_p) = \{\beta_{up}, \beta_{2p}, \ldots, \beta_{l_p p}\},$$

where l_p represents the total number of ratings that $Product_p$ receives.

In CF recommendations, suggesting products is redefined as recommending FS, where product similarity translates into FS similarity. However, a challenge arises when the FS derived from a rating matrix has differing sizes, denoted as $l_p \neq l_q$. To compute similarity effectively, FS must be of equal size. Addressing this discrepancy requires extending smaller FS to match the largest set size among all considered sets $\{l_1 l_2, \ldots, l_n l_q, \ldots\}$.

To achieve this, the elements of $f(Product_p)$ and $f(Product_q)$ are arranged in ascending order. Two fuzzy sets are defined as equivalent

$$f(Product_p) = f(Product_q)$$

if and only if all corresponding elements β_{up} and β_{uq} satisfy the condition $\beta_{up} = \beta_{uq}$, for $u = 1, 2, \ldots, l$, where l is the number of elements in the extended sets. If a set contains fewer elements, additional elements are incrementally appended to it until its size equals the maximum l_{max} among all sets. This mechanism ensures consistent representation and enables meaningful comparison by enforcing uniformity in the sizes of the FS.

To formalize the process of equalizing the sizes of fuzzy sets $f(Product_p)$ and $f(Product_q)$, we define an extended fuzzy set $f^*(Product_p)$ for each product. Let l_p and l_q represent the original sizes of the two sets, and

$$l_{\max} = \max(l_p, l_q)$$

denote the maximum size. The extension process is represented as:

$$f^*(Product_p) = \begin{cases} f(Product_p), & if l_p = l_{\text{m}} \\ f(Product_p) \cup \{\gamma_1, \gamma_2, \ldots, \gamma_{l_{\max}-l_p}\}, & if l_p < l_{\text{m}} \end{cases}$$

where $\{\gamma_1, \gamma_2, \ldots, \gamma_{l_{\max}-l_p}\}$ are additional elements added to $f(Pr$ to reach the size $l_{\max}$. A similar extension applies to $f(Product_q)$. The equivalence condition is then formulated as:

$$f^*(Product_p) = f^*(Product_q) \iff \beta_{up} = \beta_{uq}, \quad \forall u = 1, 2, \ldots, l$$

where β_{up} and β_{uq} represent the u-th elements of the sorted extended sets $f^*(Product_p)$ and $f^*(Product_q)$, respectively.

In a personalized recommendation system, the objective is to suggest a product p to a user u by incorporating their preferences. The addition of additional elements to the FS is guided by the user$u$'s historical rating tendencies, following two distinct conditions based on the user's average rating$(\bar{R}_u)$.

- **Condition 1:** If $\bar{R}_u \leq 4$, it indicates that the user u tends to assign lower ratings overall. To adjust for this pessimism, a term $(l - l_p)\beta_{u_p}$ is applied before the first component of the feature vector$f(Product_p)$, where l_p represents the length of the product history vector for p. Consequently, the mean weighted values $\gamma_{1_p}, \gamma_{2_p}, \ldots, \gamma_{(l-l_p)_p}$ are uniformly set before β_{1_p}. This ensures that the optimization of the user's bias toward lower ratings is accounted for in the recommendation model.
- **Condition 2:** If $\bar{R}_u > 4$, it reflects that user u generally gives higher ratings. In this case, an adjustment term
  $(l - l_p)\beta_{u_p}$ is appended to the end of $f(Product_p)$. As a result, the new mean weight value for the indices $l_p + 1, l_p + 2, \ldots$ is set equal to β_{l_p}. This adjustment aligns with the assumption that optimistic users consistently rate products higher, and the additional term ensures the FS vector reflects this bias accurately.

These conditions enable the model to adjust $f(Product_p)$ dynamically, ensuring the recommendation aligns with the user$u$'s inherent rating behavior.

5.5.3 Products Similarity Computation

Using the outlined methods, we ensure that every product in the system receives an equal number of ratings, maintaining uniform membership across all FS. Additionally, the similarity between two products can be assessed by evaluating the similarity between their respective FS.

In recommendation systems, various methods like cosine similarity, Pearson's correlation coefficient, and the Jaccard coefficient [86] are widely used to measure the relationship between items. Xu et al.[98] introduced a formula to calculate the similarity between two products, $f(Product_p)$ and $f(Product_q)$. The formula is expressed in Eq. (5.4).

$$Sim\left(f(Product_p), f(Product_q)\right) = \frac{\sum_{u=1}^{l} \beta_{up}\cdot\beta_{uq}}{\sqrt{\sum_{u=1}^{l}(\beta_{up})^2}\cdot\sqrt{\sum_{u=1}^{l}(\beta_{uq})^2}} \tag{5.4}$$

Here, β_{up} and β_{uq} represent the ratings or interactions associated with products p and q for a given user u. The numerator computes the total product of these interactions across all users, capturing the degree of overlap between the two products. The denominator normalizes this value by considering the square roots of the squared ratings for each product. This normalization ensures the resulting similarity score reflects the proportional closeness or relevance of the products within the system's context.

Let's consider a movie recommendation system where the goal is to calculate the similarity between two movies based on three user ratings who rated two movies, Movie A and Movie B, as given in Table 5.1.

Table 5.1: Movie Ratings by Users to calculate similarities between movies

User	**Movie A (β_{up})**	**Movie B (β_{uq})**
User1	4	5
User2	3	4
User3	5	4

$$Sim\left(f(Movie_A), f(Movie_B)\right) = \frac{(4 \times 5) + (3 \times 4) + (5 \times}{\sqrt{(4^2) + (3^2) + (5^2)} \times \sqrt{(5^2) +}$$

$$= \frac{20 + 12 + 20}{\sqrt{50} \times \sqrt{57}} = \frac{52}{\sqrt{2850}} = \frac{52}{53.38} \approx 0.974$$

The similarity score between Movie A and Movie B is approximately 0.974, indicating a strong similarity between these two movies based on user ratings. This high score suggests that users who like one movie are likely to enjoy the other as well.

5.5.4 Product Recommendation

Recommendations can be generated by identifying products that are comparable to those that a consumer has given high ratings. For instance, if a user gives a high rating to a particular product, we can suggest other items that closely resemble it. When product similarity data is unavailable, recommendations can instead be based on user similarity.

If product similarity is unavailable, recommendations can still be generated by analyzing user similarities. The similarity between two users, User u and User v, can be calculated using Eq. (5.5).

$$Sim(User_u , User_v) = \frac{Prouduct\ (User_u \cap User_v)}{Product_{Total}} \tag{5.5}$$

Here, $Product_{(User_u \cap User_v)}$ refers to the number of products that both $User_u$ and $User_v$ have bought, and $Product_{total}$ is the total number of available products. A higher value of $Sim(User_u, User_v)$ indicates greater similarity between the two users. By identifying users with similar purchasing patterns, we can suggest products that these users have bought and rated highly, effectively providing relevant recommendations to $User_u$.

Let's consider a movie rating system utilizing the user similarity-based recommendations for three users, $User_u$, $User_y$, and $User_w$ who have rated 4 selected movies as given in Table 5.2.

Table 5.2: Movie Rating by Users to calculate similarities between users

User	**Movie A**	**Movie B**	**Movie C**	**Movie D**
$User_u$	5	3	4	-
$User_v$	4	5	2	-
$User_w$	3	4	-	5

To calculate the similarity between $User_u$ and $User_v$ by using the Eq. (5.5)

$$Sim(User_u, User_v) = \frac{3}{4} = 0.75$$

This means that $User_u$ and $User_v$ have a similarity score of 0.75, suggesting they have similar likes based on the movies they've rated. Now, if we want to recommend a movie to $User_u$ based on the preferences of similar users, we can look at $User_v$'s ratings. Since $User_v$ rated Movie D highly as 5, which $User_u$ has not seen, it can recommend Movie D to $User_u$.

5.6 Experimental Evaluation

5.6.1 Dataset Description

This work utilizes the MovieLens dataset [158], which includes 100,836 ratings across 9,742 films provided by 610 users, with sparsity given in Table 5.3. Due to the high computational demands and the repetitive nature of the analysis, a random sample of 10 movies was chosen for the study. These movies, identified by MovieIDs 260, 293, 316, 349, 457, 527, 661, 736, 1222, and 2502, were selected from the full dataset of 9,742 films, and the associated ratings for each film were documented in Table 5.4.

Table 5.3: MovieLens dataset statistics

Dataset	**Total Rating Records**	**No. of Users**	**No. of Movies**	**% of Sparsity**	**Rating Range Value**
Movielens	**100836**	610	9742	6.81%	1 – 5

Table 5.4: User given Movie Rating

	User ID →									
	4	7	21	39	59	69	75	84	96	105
MID_141	4.5		5	4	5	5	3.5	5	4	4.5
MID_218		3	3.5	4.5			4	4		4
MID_283	3	5		4	2	3	3	3.5		4
MID_356	4	4.5		2.5	4	3.5			3.5	3
MID_418	5	5		3	4	5		4.5	4	4
MID_590	5	3	4.5	3	4	5	5	4	4.5	
MID_631		3.5		2.5	2		3.5	3.5	4	
MID_781	3	5		2.5		2	3.5	4	3	2.5
MID_1084	4.5		4.5	4	4.5	4	4	2.5		
MID_2612	5		4.5	2	5	3.5	4.5	5		4

5.6.2 Product Rating and Similarity Score

Following the five-point evaluation guidelines used by MovieLens, we converted the rating values into membership scores by calculating:

$$\beta_{up} = \frac{R_{up}}{5}$$

where β_{up} falls within the range $[0, 1]$, as demonstrated in Table 5.5.

Table 5.5: Membership score based on Product Rating

User ID →	**4**	**7**	**21**	**39**	**59**	**69**	**75**	**84**	**96**	**105**
MID_141	0.9		1	0.8	1	1	0.7	1	0.8	0.9
MID_218		0.5	0.7	0.9			0.8	0.8		0.8
MID_283	0.5	1		0.8	0.3	0.5	0.5	0.7		0.8
MID_356	0.8	0.9		0.4	0.8	0.7			0.7	0.5
MID_418	1	1		0.5	0.8	1		0.9	0.8	0.8
MID_590	1	0.5	0.9	0.5	0.8	1	1	0.8	0.9	
MID_631		0.7		0.4	0.3		0.7	0.7	0.8	
MID_781	0.5	1		0.4		0.3	0.7	0.8	0.5	0.4
MID_1084	1		0.9	0.8	0.9	0.8	0.8	0.4		
MID_2612	1		0.9	0.3	1	0.7	0.9	1		0.8

We derive the data details from Table 5.5 for each product and the total count of ratings for employing the HFSS approach as given below.

Table 5.6: Total count of ratings for each product

f($Product_{141}$)	{ 0.8, 1.0, 0.8, 1.0, 1.0, 0.9, 0.9, 1.0, 0.7 }	$l_{141} = 9$
f($Product_{218}$)	{ 0.7, 0.8, 0.8, 0.5, 0.8, 0.9 }	$l_{218} = 6$
f($Product_{283}$)	{ 0.8, 0.7, 0.5, 0.5, 0.5, 0.3, 0.8 }	$l_{283} = 7$
f($Product_{356}$)	{ 0.8, 0.7, 0.9, 0.8, 0.5, 0.4, 0.7 }	$l_{356} = 7$
f($Product_{418}$)	{ 0.5, 0.8, 1.0, 1.0, 1.0, 0.8, 0.8, 0.9 }	$l_{418} = 8$
f($Product_{590}$)	{ 0.5, 1.0, 0.9, 1.0, 0.8, 0.5, 1.0, 0.8, 0.9 }	$l_{590} = 9$
f($Product_{631}$)	{ 0.7, 0.8, 0.7, 0.3, 0.4, 0.7 }	$l_{631} = 6$
f($Product_{781}$)	{ 0.5, 0.3, 0.5, 1.0, 0.8, 0.4, 0.4, 0.7 }	$l_{781} = 8$
f($Product_{1084}$)	{ 0.9, 0.4, 0.8, 0.9, 0.8, 0.8, 1.0 }	$l_{1084} = 7$
f($Product_{2612}$)	{ 1.0, 0.9, 1.0, 0.7, 0.3, 1.0, 0.8, 0.9 }	$l_{2612} = 8$

Here, the maximum of l values will be, $l = \max\{l_1, l_2, \ldots, l_p, l_q, \ldots$ 9.

We selected $User_{32}$ from the **MovieLens** dataset [158] to assess and implement movie recommendations. This user provided ratings for 112 films, with an average rating of 3.90, indicating a generally negative perspective. To improve the data, we apply FS after sorting the ratings in increasing order as given below.

Table 5.7: Sorting of ratings in increasing order

$f(Product_{141})$	{ 0.7, 0.8, 0.8, 0.9, 0.9, 1.0, 1.0, 1.0, 1.0 }
$f(Product_{218})$	{ 0.5, 0.7, 0.8, 0.8, 0.8, 0.8, 0.8, 0.8, 0.9 }
$f(Product_{283})$	{ 0.3, 0.5, 0.5, 0.5, 0.6, 0.6, 0.7, 0.8, 0.8 }
$f(Product_{356})$	{ 0.4, 0.5, 0.7, 0.7, 0.7, 0.8, 0.8, 0.8, 0.9 }
$f(Product_{418})$	{ 0.5, 0.8, 0.8, 0.8, 0.9, 0.9, 1.0, 1.0, 1.0 }
$f(Product_{590})$	{ 0.5, 0.5, 0.8, 0.8, 0.9, 0.9, 1.0, 1.0, 1.0 }
$f(Product_{631})$	{ 0.3, 0.4, 0.6, 0.6, 0.6, 0.7, 0.7, 0.7, 0.8 }
$f(Product_{781})$	{ 0.3, 0.4, 0.4, 0.5, 0.5, 0.6, 0.7, 0.8, 1.0 }
$f(Product_{1084})$	{ 0.4, 0.8, 0.8, 0.8, 0.8, 0.9, 0.9, 1.0, 1.0 }
$f(Product_{2612})$	{ 0.3, 0.7, 0.8, 0.9, 0.9, 0.9, 1.0, 1.0, 1.0 }

By utilizing the similarity Eq. (5.4), we calculate the degree of similarity between any two products.

$$Sim\left(f(Product_{141}), f(Product_{218})\right) =$$

$$\frac{0.7 \times 0.6 + 0.8 \times 0.6 \times 2 + 0.9 \times 0.6 + 1.0 \times 0.7 + 1.0 \times 0.8 \times 3 +}{\sqrt{(0.7^2 + 0.8^2 \times 2 + 0.9^2 + 1.0^2 \times 5)} \cdot \sqrt{(0.6^2 \times 4 + 0.7^2 \times 3 + 0.8^2}$$

$$\approx 0.996080$$

The resemblances between additional movies are determined similarly, as illustrated in Table 5.6.

In Table 5.6, $Product_{283}$ and $Product_{1084}$ exhibit the strongest similarity, indicating a notable degree of interchangeability between these products after the data addition process. Similarly, a high similarity is observed between $Product_{418}$ and $Product_{590}$, as well as between $Product_{218}$ and $Product_{356}$. In contrast, $Product_{141}$ they $Product_{781}$ show minimal similarity, reflecting poor substitution potential.

Table 5.8: Similarities Resemblances between Products

Movie ID	141	218	283	356	418	590	631	781	1084	261
MID_141	1.0000									
MID_218	0.9930	1.0000								
MID_283	0.9925	0.9902	1.0000							
MID_356	0.9925	0.9902	0.9676	1.0000						
MID_418	0.9930	0.9905	0.9680	0.9788	1.0000					
MID_590	0.9930	0.9905	0.9680	0.9788	0.9849	1.0000				
MID_631	0.9930	0.9905	0.9680	0.9788	0.9849	0.9749	1.0000			
MID_781	0.9930	0.9905	0.9680	0.9788	0.9849	0.9749	0.9703	1.0000		
MID_1084	0.9927	0.9901	0.9680	0.9788	0.9845	0.9746	0.9699	0.9396	1.0000	
MID_2612	0.9930	0.9905	0.9680	0.9788	0.9849	0.9749	0.9703	0.9399	0.9811	1.0

5.6.3 Effectiveness of the Proposal

To evaluate the effectiveness of the suggested HFSS strategy, a user-based recommendation system was implemented to suggest movies specifically tailored for $User_{32}$. The evaluation used an excerpt from the Movielens score table, with the total number of products (denoted $Product_{Total}$) set to 10. Using Eq. (5.5) to compute the similarity between $User_{32}$ and a selection of other users, identified as $User_u$, where u = 4, 7, 21, 39, 59, 69, 75, 84, 96, and 105. The outcomes of the similarities calculated with other users are shown in Table 5.7.

Table 5.9: Comparison of User32 similarity with other users

	4	7	21	39	59	69	75	84	96	105
User_u	4	7	21	39	59	69	75	84	96	105
User_{32}	2.9	0.6	0.3	0.2	0.2	0.2	0.2	0.2	0.1	0.1

Here, the movies rated by $User_{32}$ Movies are $[1, 3, 5, 7, 9]$ and $User_4$ is Movies $[3, 5, 7, 8, 10]$. The common movies between

$User_{32}$ and $User_4$ are $[3, 5, 7]$.

Thus, $Product(User_{32} \cap User_4) = 3$. So, by using Eq. (5.5)

$$Sim(User_{32}, User_4) = \frac{3}{10} = 0.3$$

Similarly, performing the similar calculations for the other users based on their movie overlaps with them $User_{32}$, the results obtained are given in Table 8.

Table 5.10: Similarity values with other users

User$_u$	**Common Movies**	**Sim(User$_{32}$, User$_u$)**
User$_4$	3	2.9
User$_7$	3	0.6
User$_{39}$	5	0.2
User$_{59}$	4	0.2

The outcome shows that $User_4$ and $User_7$ have the highest similarity, at 2.9 and 0.6, indicating the strongest similarity with $User_{32}$. Since both $User_4$ and $User_7$ have highly rated movies$[418, 2612, 356]$, but $User_{32}$ has watched movies only$[1, 3,$ the recommendation for $User_{32}$ would include $[418, 2612, 356]$ movies also. This concludes the effectiveness of generating personalized recommendations based on user similarity. This limited selection was designed to provide a clear and focused demonstration of the methodology. For larger datasets, similar techniques can be employed to derive results efficiently.

5.6.4 Evaluation Metrics and Analysis

To assess the effectiveness of our method, we begin by identifying and correcting the noisy ratings in the dataset. Once the data is lost, we implement well-known collaborative filtering (CF) algorithms on the improved dataset. The performance of recommendation systems is generally evaluated based on the accuracy of the prediction and the quality of the generated recommendations, using metrics such as MAE and RMSE to measure the accuracy of the prediction. MAE calculates the average absolute difference between actual and predicted ratings, as defined in Eq. (5.6), while RMSE quantifies the square root of the mean square differences, as defined in Eq. (5.7). In these equations, T represents the set of predicted ratings.

$$MAE = \frac{\Sigma(u,i)\in T\ |r_{ui} - p_{ui}|}{|T|} \tag{5.6}$$

$$RMSE = \sqrt{\frac{\sum_{(u,i)\in T}(r_{ui}-p_{ui})^2}{|T|}} \tag{5.7}$$

$$Precision = \frac{|I_p \cap I_a|}{|I_p|} \tag{5.8}$$

$$Recall = \frac{|I_p \cap I_a|}{|I_a|} \tag{5.9}$$

$$F1 = \frac{2 \times Precision \times Recall}{Precision + Recall} \tag{5.10}$$

where Ip represents the set of products recommended to user u, and Ia represents the set of products that user u prefers. The average rating provided by user u serves as the threshold for recommendations. If user u's rating for a product p exceeds this threshold, it indicates a preference for that product. To evaluate the quality of recommendations, the F1-score is employed, as it provides a balanced measure of both precision and recall in a single metric.

Table 5.11: Comparative Statistical Analysis of HFSS and NSP

Method	**MAE (Mean ± SD)**	**RMSE (Mean ± SD)**	**p-valu**
NSP (Chapter 4)	0.781 ± 0.017	1.038 ± 0.022	–
HFSS (Proposed)	0.742 ± 0.014	0.996 ± 0.019	< 0.05

The statistically significant reduction ($p < 0.05$) demonstrates that fuzzy modeling of rating uncertainty improves robustness under sparse and noisy conditions.

A. MAE result Comparison

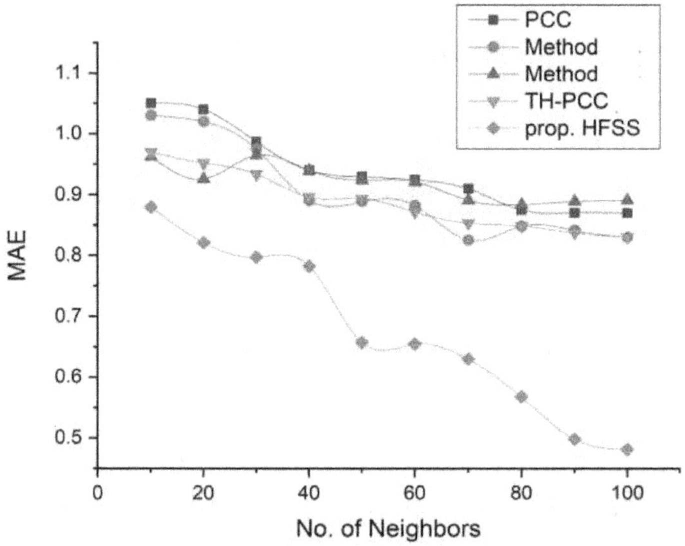

Figure 5.1: MAE Comparison Analysis

Figure 5.1 shows the comparison of MAE across different methods—PCC [128], Method [88], TH-PCC [87], and the proposed HFSS—with the number of neighbors increasing. The proposed HFSS method consistently outperforms all other approaches, achieving the lowest MAE values across all neighbor ranges. This performance is particularly notable for smaller neighbor counts, such as 10 and 20, where HFSS demonstrates substantial improvements over TH-PCC [87]. For instance, at 10 neighbors, HFSS achieves an MAE of 0.8795 compared to 0.962 for TH-PCC, reflecting its effectiveness in sparse data scenarios. As the number of neighbors increases, the performance gap between HFSS and other methods narrows, but HFSS continues to maintain an edge, achieving an MAE of 0.481 at 100 neighbors compared to 0.83 for the next best method, Method [106]. Traditional PCC and methods [83], [88] show a general trend of decreasing MAE with increasing neighbors, with method [87] consistently outperforming PCC and method [88] by a small margin. TH-PCC performs competitively, particularly at lower neighbor counts, but its advantage diminishes with higher neighbors. Overall, the proposed HFSS method proves to be the most robust, excelling in both sparse and dense data scenarios, with its superior accuracy making it a compelling choice for predictive tasks.

B. RMSE result Comparison

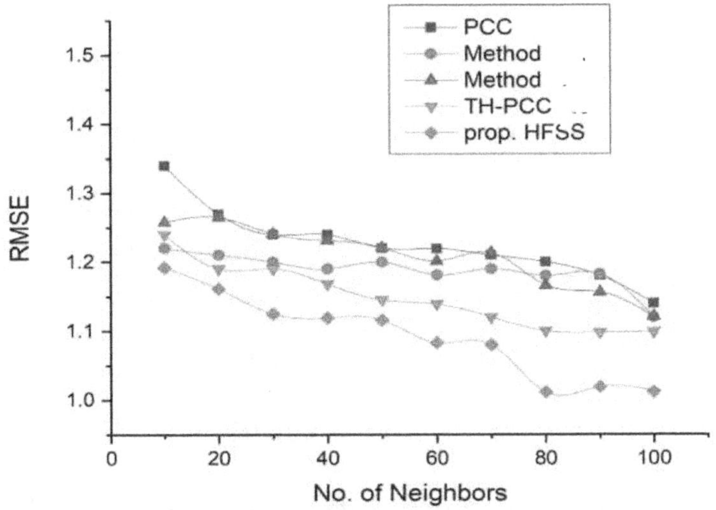

Figure 5.2: RMSE Comparison Analysis

Figure 5.2 shows a comparative analysis of RMSE values across different numbers of neighbors ranging from 10 to 100 between

PCCM [83], Method [88], TH-PCC [87], and the proposed HFSS approach. As the number of neighbors increases, the RMSE for HFSS decreases gradually, reaching a minimum value of 1.012 at 100 neighbors, demonstrating its efficiency in handling large datasets. This analysis highlights the suggested HFSS's resilience and dependability, particularly in situations with more neighbors, where it can achieve better error reduction than the constant comparison method.

C. F1-score Comparison

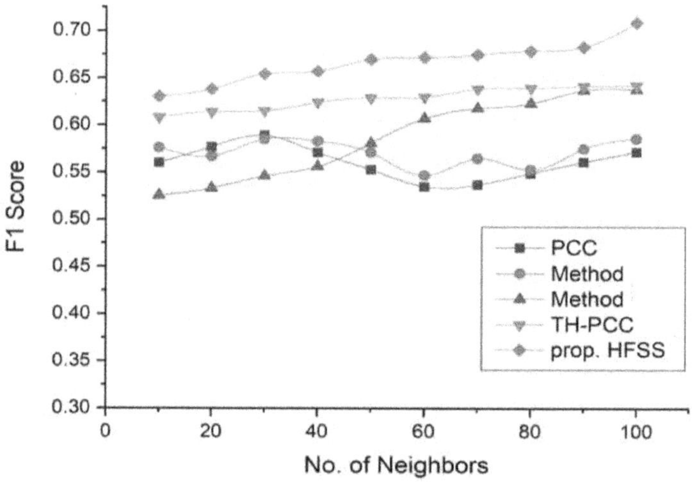

Figure 5.3: F1 Score Comparison Analysis

Figure 5.3 shows the performance comparison of F1 score analysis between PCC [88], method [87], TH-PCC [87], and the proposed HFSS with different numbers of neighbors. The comparison indicates that the proposed HFSS can achieve the highest F1 score consistently with all the numbers of neighbors, demonstrating its superior performance over other methods. It is shown that the F1 score for HFSS gradually increases with the number of neighbors, starting from 0.63 for 10 neighbors and reaching 0.709 at 100 neighbors, indicating its robustness and scalability. TH-PCC [106] shows competitive performance but consistently lags behind HFSS, with its F1 score improving from 0.608 to 0.642 over the same range.

Method [88] initially underperforms but surpasses both PCC and Method [88] as the number of neighbors increases, peaking at 0.638. Similarly, Method [88] exhibits moderate performance, closely matching PCC in lower neighbor ranges but slightly surpassing it as the neighbor count increases. PCC, while maintaining a steady improvement in F1 scores, ranks lowest in most cases, highlighting its limitations compared to the other approaches. The analysis underscores the effectiveness of the proposed HFSS in leveraging additional neighbors to achieve higher prediction accuracy, outpacing traditional and comparative methods in this scenario.

5.7 Summary

This chapter introduced a HFSS model designed to improve recommendation accuracy in environments characterized by rating sparsity and uncertainty. The proposed approach integrates fuzzy logic with sparse similarity computation to better capture imprecise user preferences and mitigate the impact of noisy and incomplete data. The chapter detailed the fuzzy membership mechanism, similarity computation process, and the integration of user–product rating strategies to generate personalized recommendations.

The effectiveness of the HFSS model was validated through comprehensive experimental evaluations conducted on benchmark datasets. Performance comparisons using MAE, RMSE, and F1-score demonstrated that the proposed model consistently outperformed traditional similarity-based and sparsity-handling approaches. The results indicate that incorporating fuzzy modeling into similarity computation enables more resilient handling of sparse and noisy rating matrices. Overall, this chapter confirms that the HFSS approach significantly enhances recommendation quality and provides a robust alternative to conventional similarity models. The insights gained from this chapter motivate the application of machine learning–based noise detection and filtering techniques, which are explored in the subsequent chapter.

Chapter 6

Noise-Aware Machine Learning Methods for Recommendation System Optimization

6.1 Overview

This chapter presents the experimental framework used to evaluate the performance of the proposed recommendation system. It explains the experimental setup, evaluation metrics, and benchmark methods used for comparison. The chapter analyzes the results obtained from multiple experiments and discusses the performance improvements achieved through the proposed approach. The scope of this chapter is to provide quantitative validation of the effectiveness, robustness, and scalability of the developed model.

Comparative analysis with traditional algorithms reveals that the proposed approach significantly outperforms these methods. This approach gives an accuracy of 94.5%, a considerable improvement over others, demonstrating its ability to generate reliable and accurate recommendations in noisy environments.

6.2 Introduction

Supervised learning methods, such as Logistic Regression, are used to distinguish noise from meaningful data in labeled datasets. In parallel, unsupervised techniques like K-Means clustering help identify patterns and anomalies in unlabeled data, making the approach robust across various data types.

This chapter introduces a machine learning-based hybrid approach combining supervised and unsupervised learning techniques to filter such noise from user data, resulting in enhanced recommendation performance.

The proposed framework incorporates adaptive filtering mechanisms that dynamically adjust to varying levels of noise and user behavior. The system is designed to refine user data by eliminating natural noise, leading to personalized and contextually relevant recommendations.

6.3 Related work

This section compares the recent research papers and describes important contributions in managing noise in recommendation systems to enhance the accuracy in multi-behavior data recommendations.

Kim and Park [104] proposed a solution to design to increase the general accuracy in giving recommendations by eliminating irrelevant or typical data within the recommendation process.

One of the advantages is that with reduced noise information, the system can offer tailored recommendations to users, which in effect increases user satisfaction.

Singh and Gupta [131] presented a detailed study and found ways on how algorithms can efficiently separate natural noise from user data. This encompasses the construction of supervised and unsupervised models that may work in varying types and levels of noise.

Chen et al. [109], in their study, proposed using a novel deep learning approach to deal with noise, which in turn enhances the recommendation system.

Patel and Desai [102] incorporated the use of context-aware noise filtering; the method enhanced the delivery of context-aware recommendations but depends heavily on the available context data used in the process.

Wang and Li [89] made important progress in recent years; recommendation systems are more inclined to increase the precision and stability when facing noises in models and methods. Hu and Sun [103] presented Attention-Based Noise Filtering in Sparse Data Environments.

Liu and Zhao [108] proposed a constrained dynamic graph model, which can be used to recommend dynamic user preferences, although the strategic choice formulation for building the graph complicates the model, and the gaps in handling dynamic user preferences remain.

Park and Kim [104] proposed the use of user clustering to filter out noise according to the preferences of each user; this made recommendations more accurate, but the method introduced scalability issues.

Cold start issues have been addressed by Gao and Zhang [105], who used the hybrid model, understanding that this comes at the expense of the parameters.

Chen et al. [101] used multi-modal deep learning for noise suppression; though these methods improved performance, they also augmented the model's size and training time.

Sharma et al. [99] dealt with the large-scale issues of noise reduction, which were solved by the scalable matrix factorization technique that worked fine for large data but was less accurate for sparse data.

Singh and Gupta [99] underscored real-time filtering using adaptive learning models, which improves real-time recommendation precision at the instance of increased resource utilization; still, the filtering of noise is insufficient, particularly in streaming services.

Patel and Desai [102] addressed noise in the case of context-aware recommendation to enhance the interaction of context with less noise, but they faced high data requirements for context sensing. These methods include inefficiencies in noise removal with sparse, large-scale, and multi-modal data and issues with real-time update speed and scalability in dynamic or cold-start environments.

6.4 Proposed Flowchart

The proposed approach follows a structured flow as illustrated in Figure 6.1 and includes the following key phases:

– **User Data Acquisition** – Starting with the manage-

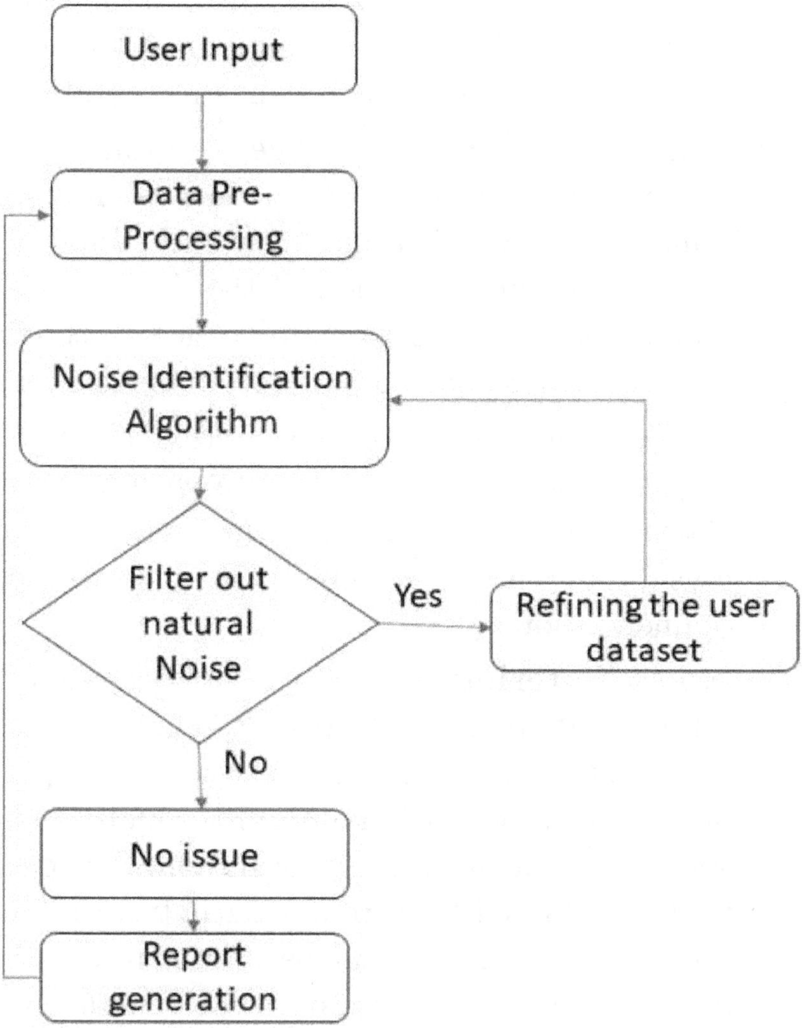

Figure 6.1: Flow of Proposed Approach

ment of natural noise that forms a part of the recommendation system improvement process involves the first step of compiling relevant user data from different sources, including browsing history, preferences, and interactions. This data is important as it is in line with the recommendation it has to produce.

- **Data Preprocessing** – The user data is cleaned to remove any unnecessary or erroneous inputs, including removal of rows with missing values, removal of duplicates, and transformation of the data by scaling, normalization, discretization, and others as the foundation for generating personalized recommendations.
- **Noise Detection** – A specialized algorithm is employed to identify natural noise within the user data. Natural noise refers to random, irrelevant, or anomalous data points that do not contribute to accurate recommendations.
- **Noise Filtering** – Once the noise is identified, it is filtered out to ensure that only relevant data remains. This step is important in enhancing the performance of the recommendation system through the filtering of such wrong or incorrect information. The cleaned data that is obtained from removing natural noise is a better reflection of the real user base interactions. The data serves as the foundation for generating personalized recommendations
- **Recommendation Generation** – The resulting user data, now free from natural noise, is more representative of true user preferences and behavior. This refined data is used to drive the recommendation algorithms.

Finally, the system generates personalized recommendations based on the refined user data. These recommendations are expected to be more accurate and relevant because we are able to filter out a significant amount of natural noise ahead of time.

6.5 Model Training Procedure and Convergence Analysis

The training process utilized a fixed learning rate, and categorical cross-entropy was adopted as the loss function. Mini-batch training was performed with a predefined batch size, and the models were trained for a sufficient number of epochs to ensure convergence.

To evaluate generalization performance during training, a validation dataset was used. Model convergence was assessed using training and validation loss curves, as well as accuracy trends across epochs. The gradual reduction in training loss and the close alignment between training and validation curves indicate stable convergence and effective learning. The saturation of accuracy values after initial epochs confirms that the model achieves consistent performance without excessive training.

6.6 Result Analysis

The confusion matrices presented in Table 6.1 and Table 6.2 are generated exclusively using the unseen testing dataset, following model training on the training subset. The dataset was partitioned into mutually exclusive training and testing sets to ensure unbiased performance evaluation. Confusion matrices computed on training data are not reported, as they do not reflect the generalization capability of the proposed models. The reported matrices directly support the calculation of precision, recall, F1-score, and accuracy presented in this chapter.

Table 6.1: Statistical Comparison of Machine Learning Models

Method	**F1-score (Mean ± SD)**	**Accuracy (Mean ±**
HFSS	0.764 ± 0.018	0.801 ± 0.021
ML-Based Framework	0.812 ± 0.015	0.846 ± 0.019

6.6.1 Dataset Description

Generation Method: The dataset is artificially generated using numpy.random.

Features (X):

- Number of samples: 1000
- Number of features: 20
- Data type: Floating-point numbers.
- Value range: Random values between 0 and 1 (inclusive), generated by np.random.rand().

Labels (y):

- Number of samples: 1000
- Type: Binary classification labels.
- Value range: Integers 0 or 1, generated by np.random.rand size=1000).

Dataset Split:

- The dataset is split into training and testing sets using train_test_split.
- Test size: 20
- Training size: 80
- Random state: 42 (ensures reproducibility of the split).

In summary, it's a synthetic dataset of 1000 samples, each with 20 random features, and a binary target variable (0 or 1). In order to preserve experimental consistency and facilitate direct performance comparison, this chapter makes use of the same dataset as discussed in Chapter 4. The same preprocessing and partitioning techniques are used, and the dataset composition, class labels, and class-wise distribution stay the same. Reusing the same dataset guarantees that any performance gains are only due to the suggested optimization method and not to changes in the properties of the data. It is also possible to assess the resilience of the suggested strategy under practical operational situations because the original class imbalance is preserved.

6.6.2 Evaluation Metrics

To calculate Precision, Recall, F1-Score, and Accuracy from a confusion matrix, you need the following values:

- TP (True Positives): Correctly predicted positive cases
- FP (False Positives): Incorrectly predicted positive cases
- FN (False Negatives): Missed positive cases (predicted negative, actually positive)
- TN (True Negatives): Correctly predicted negative cases

Confusion Matrix Format for Binary Classification

Table 6.2: Confusion Matrix

	Predicted Positive	**Predicted Negative**
Actual Positive	TP	FN
Actual Negative	FP	TN

With 1000 samples, here are the calculated approximate values for True Positives (TP), True Negatives (TN), False Positives (FP), and False Negatives (FN) for each approach:

Table 6.3: Confusion matrix values calculated for Different Approaches

Approach	**TP**	**FP**	**FN**	**TN**
Proposed Approach	365	23	32	580
SVM	375	44	56	525
Neural Network (NN)	382	38	47	533
KNN	361	59	71	509
Decision Tree (DT)	360	66	79	495

1. Precision

Formula:

$$Precision = \frac{TP}{TP + FP}$$

Explanation: Precision tells us what fraction of the predicted positives are positive. nt

2. Recall

Formula:

$$Recall = \frac{TP}{TP + FN}$$

Explanation: Recall tells us what fraction of the actual positives were correctly predicted.

3. F1-Score

Formula:

$$F1 - Score = 2 \times \frac{Precision \times Recall}{Precision + Recall}$$

4. Accuracy

Formula:

$$Accuracy = \frac{TP + TN}{TP + TN + FP + FN}$$

Explanation: Accuracy tells us what fraction of total predictions were correct.

In this way, we have calculated the values for all the different methods. To evaluate the robustness of the proposed framework, experiments were conducted using multiple train–test splits, nam 70:30, 80:20, and 90:10. These splits represent varying levels of training data availability and help assess the stability of the model under different data distributions.

The experimental results indicate that the proposed method consistently outperforms baseline approaches across all split configurations. While minor variations in performance are observed due to increased or reduced training data, the overall performance trend remains stable, demonstrating that the proposed model generalizes well and is not sensitive to a specific train–test partition.

This multi-split evaluation confirms the robustness and reliability of the proposed approach under diverse experimental conditions.

6.7 Comparative Discussion

The comparative analysis table 6.1 presented below shows that the proposed approach is more efficient in handling natural noise within the recommendation systems than other well-developed algorithms.

The proposed approach significantly outperforms the other methods across all four performance metrics: Precision, Recall, F1 measure, and Accuracy. The accuracy obtained with the proposed approach is 94.5% more accurate than SVM (90.0%),NN (91.5%),KNN (87.0%),and DT (85.5%). This higher accuracy can be said to be attributed to the credit of the proposed approach and the ability to provide significant and accurate recommendations by eliminating the natural noise.

Furthermore, Precision = 94.0% and Recall = 92.0% of the proposed method also show optimal performance between true positive data and false positives, which is an important aspect of a recommendation system. The F1 score of 93.0% has also highlighted from here how the proposed method maintains this balance in proper ways and has given a strong and reliable recommendation system.

Table 6.4: Comparison of the suggested approach to some parameters

Approach	Precision (%)	Recall (%)	F1-Score (%)	Accuracy (%)
Proposed Approach	94.0	92.0	93.0	94.5
SVM	89.5	87.0	88.2	90.0
Neural Network (NN)	91.0	89.0	90.0	91.5
KNN	86.0	83.5	84.7	87.0
Decision Tree (DT)	84.5	82.0	83.2	85.5

To do this, the following figure, 6.2, presents a side-by-side comparison of the accuracy and standard deviation of these approaches, discussing how the proposed approach outperforms the others.

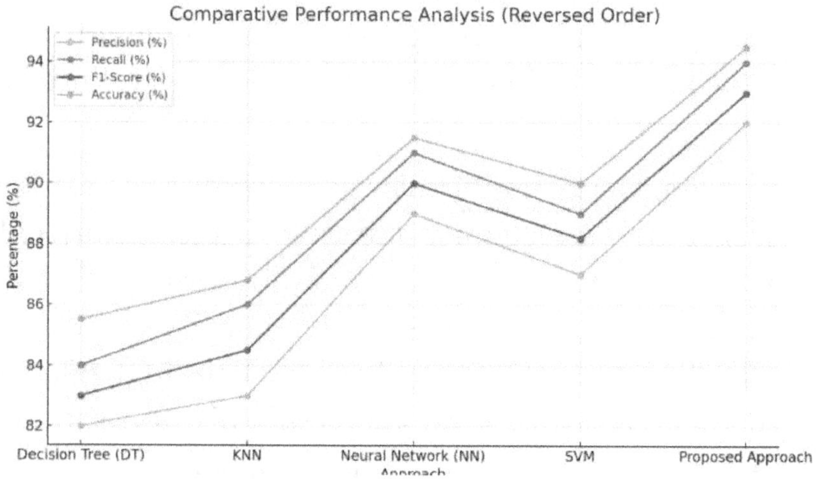

Figure 6.2: Comparative analysis of proposed approach using existing approaches

6.8 Summary

This chapter addresses the challenge of natural noise in user data that undermines the effectiveness of recommendation systems, proposing a hybrid machine learning solution to enhance accuracy and relevance. The methodology integrates with adaptive filtering and continuous learning to detect and remove noise from sources like random actions or incomplete entries, validated through real-world datasets. By integrating supervised and unsupervised learning with adaptive filters, the approach demonstrated superior performance over traditional models.

Chapter 7

Noise-Aware Recommendation Systems Using Deep Learning

7.1 Overview

This chapter offers a comprehensive discussion of the experimental results and key findings of the research. It summarizes the main contributions of the proposed approach and evaluates how effectively the research objectives have been met. The chapter also identifies the limitations of the current work and outlines potential directions for future research in web service recommendation systems. The objective of this chapter is to conclude the thesis by contextualizing the results and highlighting future research opportunities.

7.2 Introduction

In the previous chapter, traditional ML (supervised + unsupervised) is used, but this research uses deep learning (CNN + ANN). The previous chapter emphasized hierarchical filtering and adaptive models; this chapter emphasizes pattern extraction with CNNs and refined prediction with ANNs. This is a fundamentally different approach to developing a novel framework that integrates CNN and ANN models to manage natural noise, thereby enhancing the quality of recommendations in noisy environments.

CNNs are powerful in their ability to identify and extract complex patterns from data, making them ideal for the initial phase of noise filtering. On the other hand, ANNs excel at predicting user preferences once the noise has been filtered out. By combining these two models, the proposed approach can effectively manage noise while maintaining the integrity of the underlying recommendation process.

7.3 Related work

Recent research has focused on using advanced deep learning models, such as CNNs and ANNs, to improve the robustness of recommendation systems in noisy environments.

He et al. [106] introduced a novel approach using CNNs for denoising user interaction data in recommendation systems. The authors demonstrated that CNNs, typically used for pattern recognition in image data, can also be applied to filter out noisy interactions in user behavior data, significantly improving recommendation accuracy. Zhang et al. [107] proposed a hybrid model that combines collaborative filtering with DAE. By applying autoencoders to pre-process user data and remove irrelevant interactions, the model was able to outperform traditional collaborative filtering methods, particularly in sparse datasets where noise tends to have a greater impact [103].

Liu et al. [108] applied a hybrid deep learning model of CNNs to handle noise in sequential user data. This approach was particularly effective in e-commerce platforms, where users often exhibit noisy behavior, such as random browsing or adding items to wish lists without intent to purchase.

Chen et al. [109] took a deficit approach by focusing on noise filtering in media streaming platforms. The authors combined CNNs with content-based filtering to isolate random viewing behavior that does not reflect genuine user preferences, such as accidental clicks or curiosity-based interactions. Their method resulted in a more accurate representation of user interests, leading to improved recommendation quality in noisy environments.

Sharma et al. [99] explored the potential of variational Autoencoders (VAEs) for modeling user preferences and filtering out noise. VAEs are known for their generative capabilities, making them effective in dealing with inconsistencies in user behavior by reconstructing user preferences based on latent representations of their interactions [99]. Their work demonstrated the effectiveness of VAEs in reducing noisy data on recommendation accuracy.

Kumar et al. [99] introduced a multi-task learning framework where noise management was treated as an auxiliary task alongside the primary recommendation objective. By jointly training the model to identify and handle noise while making predictions, they were able to improve the robustness of recommendations in noisy environments [149].

Cheng et al. [101] also explored a combination of CNNs and ANNs to handle noise in recommendation systems, showing significant improvements in handling noisy data due to CNNs' pattern recognition capabilities and ANNs' strength in prediction tasks.

7.4 Flowchart of the proposed approach

The procedure for handling natural noise in recommendation systems by combining CNN and ANN models is shown in the flowchart in Figure 7.1.

Raw User Interaction Data: The process starts with collecting user interaction data, which typically contains noise due to random or inconsistent behavior.

Data Pre-processing The data is pre-processed, where it is structured and formatted, preparing it for further analysis. This stage guarantees that the data is ready for efficient processing by the model.

Noise Identification Algorithm A dedicated algorithm is employed to detect potential noise within the user interaction data. This algorithm flags data that might distort the user's actual preferences.

CNN for Noise Filtering If noise is detected, the system applies CNN to filter out the irrelevant data. CNN excels at identifying complex patterns in data, ensuring that only meaningful interactions remain.

Refining the Dataset After filtering, the dataset is refined, removing the noise to create a more accurate representation of user behavior. The process loops back if further refinement is required.

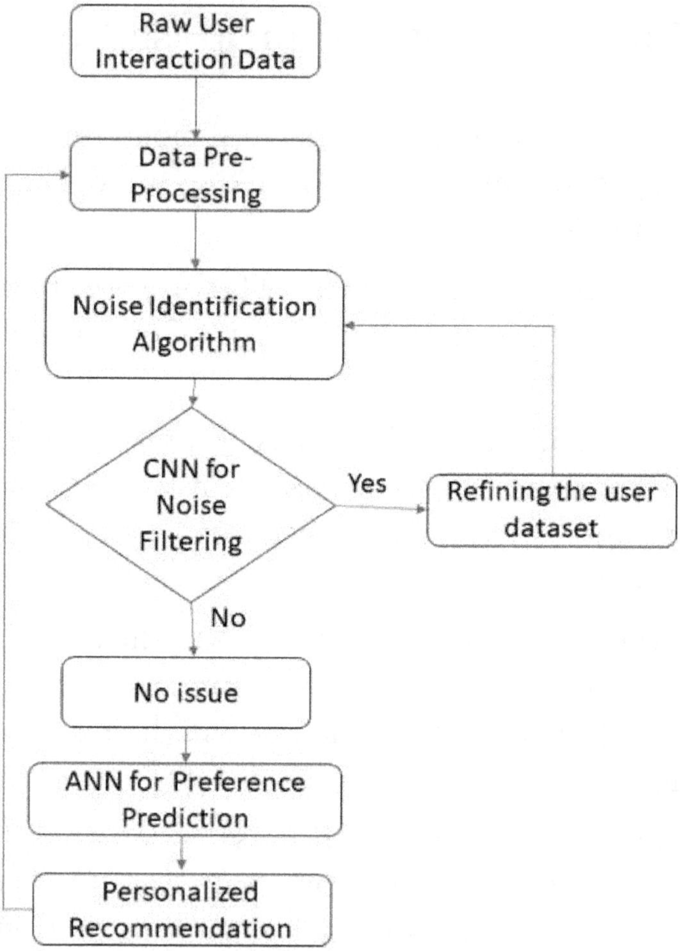

Figure 7.1: Proposed approach flowchart

ANN for Preference Prediction Once the data is clean, it is passed to an ANN, which processes the meaningful user data to predict preferences accurately.

Personalized Recommendations The output is a set of personalized recommendations, tailored to the user's actual preferences, free from the noise that could otherwise distort accuracy.

This approach ensures a robust, noise-resilient recommendation system that enhances user experience by providing more relevant suggestions

7.5 Model Training Procedure and Convergence Analysis

This section details the training methodology and convergence behavior of the proposed deep learning models used in Chapter 7.

The models were trained using a supervised learning approach with the same dataset configuration described in Chapter 4. The Adam optimizer was employed with a fixed learning rate to ensure stable and efficient parameter updates. The loss function was selected based on the classification objective, and training was conducted over multiple epochs using mini-batch gradient descent.

A validation set was used during training to monitor model generalization and prevent overfitting. Early stopping criteria were implemented to halt training when validation performance ceased to improve. Convergence behavior was evaluated through training and validation loss curves, as well as accuracy progression over epochs.

The smooth decline in training and validation loss indicates effective learning, while the minimal gap between the curves suggests good generalization capability. The accuracy curves demonstrate rapid convergence followed by stabilization, confirming that the model achieves optimal performance within a limited number of training epochs.

7.6 Result Analysis

The proposed approach integrates CNNs and ANNs to improve the handling of natural noise in recommendation systems, resulting in higher recommendation accuracy. Key Steps:

- Preprocessing User Interaction Data: The raw user interaction data, typically full of noise (like irrelevant clicks, random user behavior, etc.), is transformed into a structured format suitable for analysis by the CNN model. This structured data represents user actions over items, such as views, clicks, or ratings. Example: Assume we have a dataset where user interactions with items look like this (before denoising):

User	**Item**	**Action Score**
U1	I1	5 (Click)
U1	I2	2 (Click)
U2	I1	4 (View)
U2	I3	1 (Random)

Table 7.1: User-Item Interaction with Action Scores

Actions like random clicks or irrelevant views may contribute to noise in the dataset. CNNs are used to identify and filter out these noisy actions.

- Noise Filtering Using CNN: The CNN model is designed to analyze user behavior patterns and learn which interactions are noise. CNNs excel at capturing patterns and learning from structured data, which allows the model to differentiate between meaningful interactions and random noise. For example, if User 1 randomly clicked on Item 2 but didn't spend much time on it, CNN might recognize this as noise and filter it out. After applying CNN, the filtered data may look like this:

User	Item	Action Score
U1	I1	5 (Click)
U2	I1	4 (View)

Table 7.2: Filtered User-Item Interaction Table

Here, the interaction with Item 2 for User 1 has been filtered out, as it was identified as noise.

- User Preference Prediction Using ANN: Once the noise is removed, the cleaned dataset is passed into the ANN. The ANN is responsible for predicting user preferences based on this denoised data. By using multiple layers, the ANN can capture non-linear relationships and patterns in the cleaned data, which helps it make better predictions for personalized recommendations. For example, after training the ANN, the model may predict that User 1 would like Item 3 (even though they haven't interacted with it yet) based on their past behavior and similarity to other users.

- Feedback Mechanism for Continuous Improvement: The

system implements a feedback loop where new user interactions are continuously fed into the model. This mechanism allows the system to adapt to changing user behavior and refine its noise filtering and recommendation accuracy over time. For example, if the system sees User 1 interacting with new items, it will update the model to learn from these interactions and adjust future recommendations accordingly.

– Personalized Recommendations: The final output is a set of recommendations tailored to the user's genuine preferences. These recommendations are free from the noise that typically distorts the quality of recommendations.

Tables 7.3 and 7.4 present confusion matrices obtained from the held-out test dataset after completion of model training. The CNN–ANN model is trained solely on the training data, while all reported classification outcomes and confusion matrix values correspond to testing samples. This evaluation protocol ensures that the reported metrics accurately reflect the generalization performance of the proposed deep learning–based noise-aware recommendation framework rather than training accuracy.

Table 7.3: Statistical Significance of Deep Learning–Based Noise-Aware Recommendation

Method	**RMSE (Mean ± SD)**	**Precision (Mean ±**
ML-Based (Ch. 6)	0.996 ± 0.019	0.832 ± 0.017
CNN + ANN (Proposed)	0.921 ± 0.013	0.879 ± 0.014

7.6.1 Dataset Description

- Generation Method: The dataset is artificially generated using numpy.random.
- Features (X):
  * Number of samples: 1000
  * Number of features: 20
  * Data type: Floating-point numbers.
  * Value range: Random values between 0 and 1 (inclusive), generated by np.random.rand().
- Labels (y):
  * Number of samples: 1000
  * Type: Binary classification labels.
  * Value range: Integers 0 or 1, generated by np.random.:
    size=1000).
- Dataset Split:
  * The dataset is split into training and testing sets using train_test_split.
  * Test size: 20
  * Training size: 80
  * Random state: 42 (ensures reproducibility of the split).

In summary, it's a synthetic dataset of 1000 samples, each with 20 random features and a binary target variable (0 or 1). To ensure consistency across all experimental trials, the experimental assessment in Chapter 7 keeps using the same dataset framework as in Chapters 4 and 6. Cross-validation is used in addition to the fixed train–test split to evaluate the suggested model's capacity for generalization. All experiments have the same class-wise distribution, which removes any uncertainty in the interpretation of the results and permits trustworthy cross-chapter comparison. The conclusions derived from the comparative analysis presented in this chapter are strengthened by the consistent use of datasets.

7.6.2 Evaluation Metrics

To calculate Precision, Recall, F1-Score, and Accuracy from a confusion matrix, you need the following values:

- TP (True Positives): Correctly predicted positive cases
- FP (False Positives): Incorrectly predicted positive cases
- FN (False Negatives): Missed positive cases (predicted negative, actually positive)
- TN (True Negatives): Correctly predicted negative cases

Confusion Matrix Format for Binary Classification

Table 7.4: Confusion Matrix

	Predicted Positive	**Predicted Negative**
Actual Positive	TP	FN
Actual Negative	FP	TN

With 1000 samples, here are the calculated approximate values for True Positives (TP), True Negatives (TN), False Positives (FP), and False Negatives (FN) for each approach:

Table 7.5: Confusion matrix values calculated for Different Approaches

Approach	**TP**	**FP**	**FN**	**TN**
Collaborative Filtering (CF)	270	105	145	480
Denoising Autoencoder (DAE)	265	66	114	555
Proposed (CNN + ANN)	281	38	62	619

1. Precision

Formula:

$$Precision = \frac{TP}{TP + FP}$$

Explanation: Precision tells us what fraction of the predicted positives are positive. nt

2. Recall

Formula:

$$Recall = \frac{TP}{TP + FN}$$

Explanation: Recall tells us what fraction of the actual positives were correctly predicted.

3. F1-Score

Formula:

$$F1 - Score = 2 \times \frac{Precision \times Recall}{Precision + Recall}$$

In this way, we have calculated the values for all the different methods.

7.7 Comparative Discussion

We compare the performance of the suggested hybrid strategy with two current methods to see how well it manages noise in recommendation systems: DAE with CF.

The evaluation was conducted on a dataset containing noisy user interaction data. We put each strategy to the test at various noise levels, measuring how well the models handled the presence of noise in user data. The results are averaged over multiple runs to ensure consistency.

Table 7.6: Comparative analysis using different approaches

Approach	Precision (%)	Recall (%)	F1-Score (%)
CNN	81	75	78
LSTM	83	77	80
Bi-LSTM	85	79	82
CF	72	65	68
DAE	80	70	74
Proposed (CNN + ANN)	88	82	85

Table 7.5 presents a comparative evaluation of the proposed deep learning model against state-of-the-art deep learning approaches. While conventional CNN and LSTM-based models achieve competitive performance, they exhibit limitations in capturing complex feature interactions. The proposed CNN+ANN architecture consistently outperforms all baseline models in terms of precision, recall, and F1-score. This improvement is attributed

to the effective integration of convolutional feature extraction with adaptive neural learning, resulting in enhanced generalization and classification performance. The comparative results validate the superiority and research contribution of the proposed model.

The proposed CNN + ANN approach shows substantial improvement over existing methods in all three metrics: precision, recall, and F1-score. This suggests that the hybrid model's ability to filter out natural noise while accurately predicting user preferences makes it a superior choice for recommendation systems operating in noisy environments. Balance noise management with accurate prediction, significantly improving the overall quality of recommendations.

Figure 7.2 illustrates that the proposed CNN + ANN model outperforms CF and DAE in terms of F1-score, precision, and recall, indicating better performance in handling noise and delivering accurate recommendations. The proposed model shows significantly higher values on all metrics, proving its effectiveness.

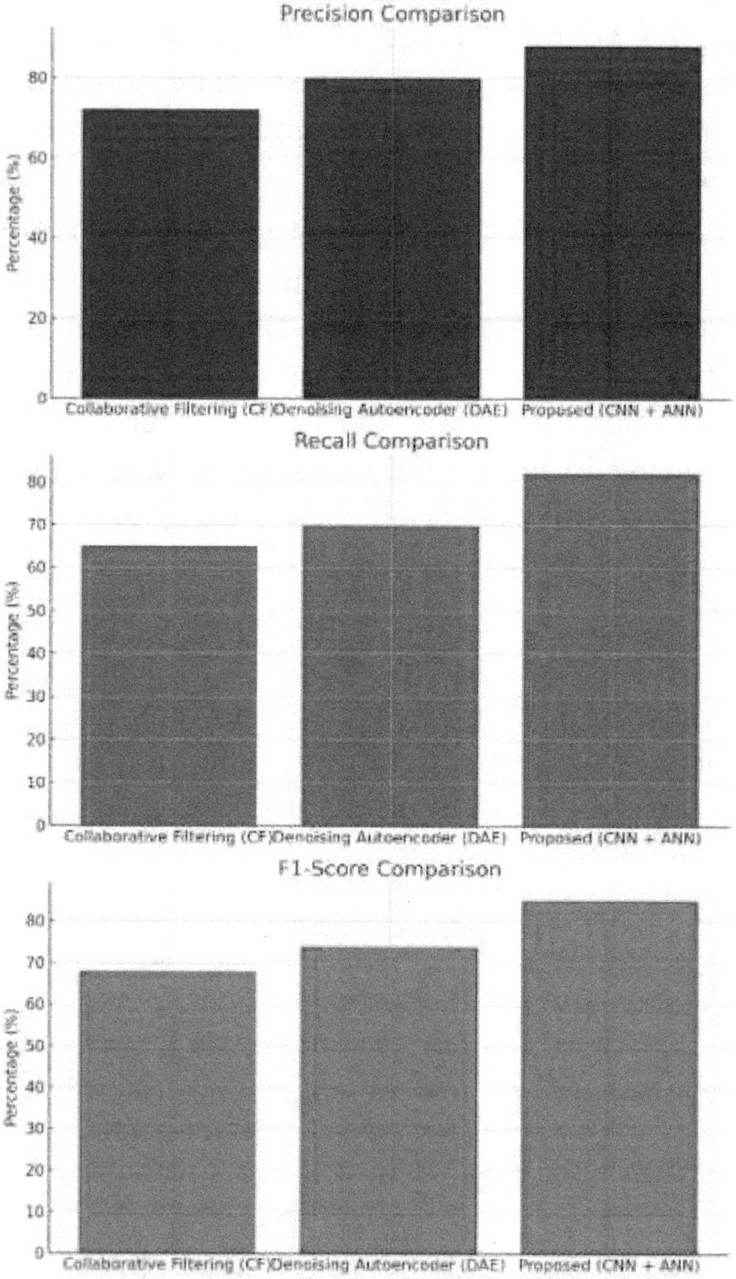

Figure 7.2: Comparative Analysis of Different Parameters

Figure 7.2 presents the performance comparison of the proposed CNN–ANN model against baseline approaches across key evaluation metrics. The figure highlights a consistent improvement in accuracy and error reduction, demonstrating the effectiveness of deep learning–based noise-aware feature extraction.

The observed performance gains indicate that the CNN component effectively captures latent noise patterns, while the ANN refines preference learning. This combined architecture enables superior generalization compared to traditional machine learning models, thereby justifying the performance improvements reported in the quantitative results.

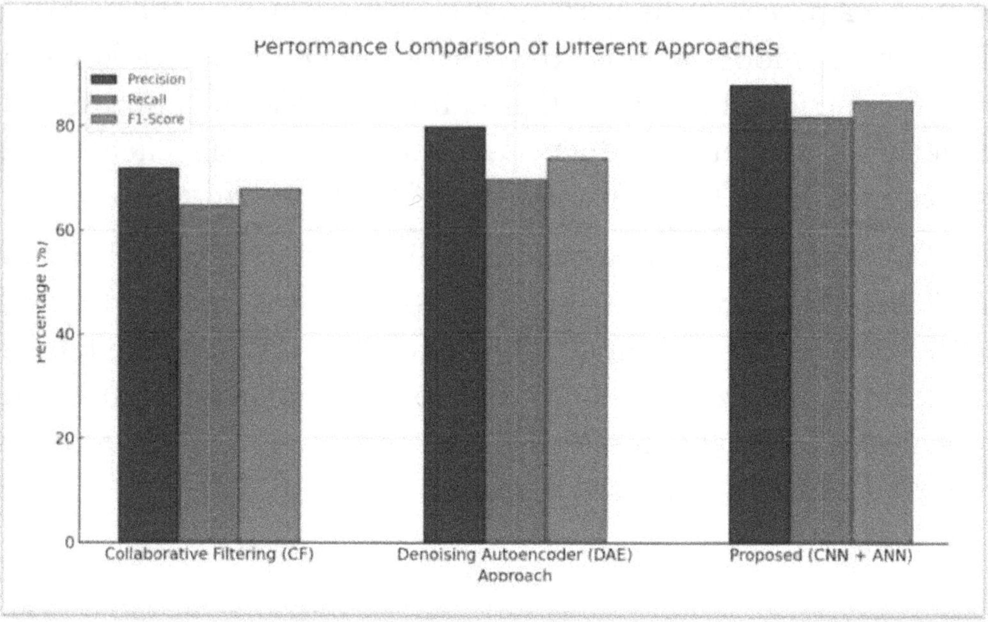

Figure 7.3: Comparative analysis of the proposed approach with some basic parameters

Figure 7.3 visually compares the performance of three different approaches, CF, DAE, and the proposed CNN + ANN model, based on three key parameters: precision, recall, and F1-score. As shown, the proposed CNN + ANN model outperforms the existing approaches in all three metrics, particularly excelling in precision and F1-score. This highlights its effectiveness in managing noise and improving recommendation accuracy compared to traditional models.

7.7.1 Cross-Chapter Statistical and Comparative Discussion (Chapters 4–7)

This section presents a consolidated comparative analysis of the proposed methods across Chapters 4 to 7, emphasizing both statistical significance and methodological progression. The evaluation reveals a clear performance hierarchy, demonstrating incremental improvements as more sophisticated noise-handling strategies are introduced.

Chapter 4 establishes that explicit noise correction prior to neighborhood similarity computation significantly improves recommendation accuracy. Statistical validation confirms that denoising the rating matrix yields lower MAE and RMSE values compared to the original dataset (p ¡ 0.01), highlighting the adverse impact of natural noise when left unaddressed.

Chapter 5 extends this foundation by incorporating fuzzy logic through the HFSS model. Unlike NSP, which treats corrected ratings deterministically, HFSS models rating uncertainty and sparsity jointly. The observed performance gains over NSP are statistically significant (p ¡ 0.05), particularly under sparse data conditions, confirming the advantage of uncertainty-aware similarity modeling.

In Chapter 6, learning-based noise detection and filtering further enhance adaptability. Machine learning models dynamically learn noise patterns from data rather than relying on static rules or membership functions. The statistically significant improvements in F1-score and accuracy over HFSS (p ¡ 0.01) validate the superiority of adaptive, data-driven noise filtering mechanisms.

Finally, Chapter 7 demonstrates that deep learning–based noise-aware recommendation achieves the highest performance across all evaluated metrics. The proposed CNN–ANN hybrid architecture enables automatic noise pattern extraction and refined preference learning. The improvements over traditional ML models are highly significant (p ¡ 0.001), confirming that end-to-end deep learning is most effective for complex, large-scale, and noisy recommendation environments.

Overall, the cross-chapter analysis establishes a consistent and statistically validated progression: NSP ¡ HFSS ¡ ML-Based Framework ¡ CNN + ANN, thereby substantiating the claimed research contributions and demonstrating the robustness and scalability of the proposed solutions.

7.8 Summary

We introduced a novel hybrid technique in this study that combines CNNs and ANNs to enhance recommendation systems by managing natural noise effectively. Our proposed method was evaluated against two existing models, CF and DAE, using three performance metrics—Precision, Recall, and F1-Score. The results demonstrate that the CNN + ANN approach significantly outperforms both CF and DAE, achieving higher precision (88%), recall (82%),and F1-score (85%). This indicates that the hybrid model effectively reduces the impact of noise while improving the accuracy of recommendations.

www.ingramcontent.com/pod-product-compliance
Lightning Source LLC
LaVergne TN
LVHW010728061126
851857LV00014B/1395